Hauling Success: A Step-by-Step Guide to Starting and Scaling Your Trucking Business

Content

Chapter 1. **Introduction:**
Understanding the Trucking Industry and Your Place in It

Chapter 2. **Developing a Business Plan:**
Setting Objectives and Charting a Path to Success

Chapter 3. **Financing Your Trucking Business:**
Securing the Funds You Need to Launch and Grow

Chapter 4. **Choosing the Right Vehicles and Equipment for Your Business**

Chapter 5. **Establishing Operations and Logistics:** Streamlining Your Fleet and Routes

Chapter 6. **Building a Strong Team:**
Hiring and Managing Drivers and Support Staff

Chapter 7. **Marketing Your Trucking Business:**
Reaching Out to Customers and Building Your Brand

Chapter 8. **Navigating Regulatory Requirements:** Understanding Federal and State Regulations

Chapter 9. **Protecting Your Business:** Insuring Your Fleet and Managing Risk

Chapter 10. **Building Strong Customer Relationships:** Providing Exceptional Service and Earning Loyalty

Chapter 11. **Optimizing Your Route Planning and Scheduling:** Enhancing Efficiency and Reducing Costs

Chapter 12. **Maximizing Load Capacity and Utilization:** Making the Most of Your Fleet's Potential

Chapter 13. **Implementing Technology Solutions:** Automating Processes and Improving Operations

Chapter 14. **Handling Disputes and Resolving Conflicts:** Dealing with Customer Complaints and Other Challenges

Chapter 15. **Expanding Your Fleet:** Scaling Your Operations and Growing Your Business

Chapter 16. **Navigating the Freight Market:** Understanding Trends and Making Smart Decisions

Chapter 17. **Developing a Safety Culture:** Protecting Your Drivers and Ensuring Compliance

Chapter 18. **Staying Ahead of the Competition:** Monitoring and Responding to Market Changes

Chapter 19. **Streamlining Dispatch and Communications:** Improving Communication and Enhancing Customer Service

Chapter 20. **Managing Fuel Costs and Efficiency:** Reducing Costs and Improving Performance

Chapter 21. **Implementing Driver Incentives and Rewards:** Motivating Your Team and Improving Retention

Chapter 22. **Understanding Taxes and Recordkeeping:** Managing Your Financials and Staying Compliant

Chapter 23. **Building Strong Relationships with Suppliers and Partners:**
Ensuring Reliable Supply Chains

Chapter 24. **Managing Maintenance and Repairs:**
Maintaining Your Fleet and Minimizing Downtime

Chapter 25. **Improving Logistics and Supply Chain Management:**
Enhancing Operations and Reducing Costs

Chapter 26. **Evaluating and Negotiating Contracts:**
Securing the Best Deals and Building Strong Partnerships

Chapter 27. **Enhancing Customer Service:**
Responding to Customer Needs and Delivering Exceptional Experiences

Chapter 28. **Building Strong Community Relationships:**
Engaging with Local Stakeholders and Building Your Reputation

Chapter 29. **Diversifying Your Business:**
Expanding Your Operations and Offering Additional Services

Chapter 30. **Attracting and Retaining Drivers:**
Providing Competitive Compensation and Benefits

Chapter 31. **Navigating Labor Relations:**
Managing Your Workforce and Avoiding Disputes

Chapter 32. **Managing Equipment Leasing and Rentals:**
Making the Most of Your Fleet and Reducing Costs

Chapter 33. **Staying Ahead of Industry Trends:**
Monitoring Changes and Adapting to Meet the Needs of Your Business

Chapter 34. **Utilizing Analytics and Performance Metrics:**
Tracking Progress and Improving Operations

Chapter 35. **Managing and Reducing Operating Costs:**
Controlling Expenses and Improving Your Bottom Line

Chapter 36. **Implementing Training and Professional Development Programs:**

Developing Your Team and Improving Performance

Chapter 37. **Building Strong Relationships with Shippers:**

Ensuring Repeat Business and Building Your Brand

Chapter 38. **Developing a Succession Plan:**

Preparing for the Future and Ensuring Continuity

Chapter 39. **Navigating Legal Issues and Compliance:**

Staying Abreast of Changes and Ensuring Compliance

Chapter 40. **Conclusion:**

Moving Forward with Confidence and Building a Thriving Trucking

Chapter 1.

Introduction

Introduction: Understanding the Trucking Industry and Your Place in It

Starting a trucking business can be an exciting and rewarding venture, but it also requires careful planning, preparation, and attention to detail. Whether you're an experienced trucker looking to go into business for yourself or a newcomer to the industry, there are many factors to consider when launching a successful trucking company.

The trucking industry is an essential component of the global economy, playing a critical role in the transportation of goods and products across borders and throughout the world. In the United States alone, trucking is a multi-billion-dollar industry, with thousands of companies operating across the country. The demand for trucking services is only growing, as businesses and consumers rely increasingly on fast, efficient, and reliable delivery options.

If you're considering starting a trucking business, it's important to understand the current state of the industry, the challenges and opportunities you'll face, and the steps you'll need to take to be successful. This guide is designed to provide a comprehensive overview of the trucking business, from developing a business plan to financing your operations and building your brand.

To get started, let's take a closer look at the trucking industry and the role of trucking companies.

The Trucking Industry and Your Role as a Trucking Company

The trucking industry is an incredibly diverse and complex sector, with companies operating in many different niches and markets. Some trucking companies specialize in hauling heavy freight and construction materials, while others focus on delivering consumer goods, food, and other products. Some trucking companies serve a local or regional market, while others operate on a national or even international scale.

Regardless of the type of trucking company you choose to start, your role will be to provide essential transportation services, ensuring that goods and products are delivered quickly, safely, and efficiently. You'll need to manage a fleet of vehicles, hire and train drivers, establish operations and logistics, and build strong relationships with customers and suppliers.

As the owner of a trucking business, you'll be responsible for making strategic decisions, managing finances and operations, and building a strong brand and reputation. You'll need to stay up-to-date on the latest trends and developments in the trucking industry, and be prepared to navigate the challenges and opportunities that arise as you grow your business.

Key Considerations When Starting a Trucking Business

Starting a trucking business requires careful planning and preparation. Here are some of the key considerations to keep in mind as you launch your business:

1. Business Plan: Develop a comprehensive business plan that outlines your objectives, strategies, and goals. This

will help you stay focused and organized as you build and grow your trucking company.

2. Financing: Secure the funding you need to launch and grow your trucking business. Consider options like loans, grants, and investments to get your business up and running.

3. Vehicles and Equipment: Choose the right vehicles and equipment for your business, taking into account factors like capacity, fuel efficiency, and cost.

4. Operations and Logistics: Establish operations and logistics that are efficient, streamlined, and cost-effective.

5. Team: Build a strong team of drivers, support staff, and managers who can help you run your business and provide excellent customer service.

6. Marketing: Develop a marketing plan that reaches out to customers and builds your brand. Utilize digital and traditional marketing strategies to reach your target audience.

7. Regulatory Requirements: Stay up-to-date on federal and state regulations, including licensing, insurance, and safety requirements.

8. Risk Management: Implement a risk management plan to protect your business against potential liabilities, accidents, and losses.

9. Customer Service: Provide excellent customer service to build strong relationships with your clients. Respond to

customer needs and inquiries promptly and professionally.

10. Technology: Embrace technology to streamline your operations, improve communication and efficiency, and increase productivity. Consider options like GPS tracking, dispatch software, and mobile apps to help you run your business more effectively.

11. Networking: Build a network of industry contacts, including suppliers, customers, and other trucking companies. Attend trade shows and conferences, and participate in industry groups and organizations.

12. Insurance: Invest in adequate insurance coverage to protect your business against potential losses and lawsuits.

13. Maintenance and Repairs: Establish a maintenance and repair plan to keep your vehicles and equipment in top condition and reduce downtime.

14. Fuel Management: Implement a fuel management plan to control fuel costs and improve efficiency.

15. Driver Management: Recruit, train, and retain quality drivers to ensure safe and efficient deliveries. Offer competitive compensation packages and benefits, and foster a positive work environment.

16. Load Management: Develop a load management plan that maximizes your capacity and reduces costs. Optimize your routes, schedules, and loads to minimize waste and maximize profits.

17. Dispatching: Implement a dispatch system that streamlines communication and reduces downtime. Ensure that your dispatch team is trained and equipped to handle the demands of your business.

18. Record-keeping: Maintain accurate and comprehensive records of your financial transactions, expenses, and operations. Utilize accounting software and other tools to help you manage your records.

19. Safety: Foster a culture of safety in your trucking business, and comply with all federal and state safety regulations. Ensure that your vehicles and equipment are maintained to the highest standards, and invest in safety training for your drivers.

20. Customer Relationships: Maintain positive relationships with your customers by providing reliable and efficient service. Respond promptly to customer inquiries and complaints, and seek feedback to continually improve your services.

21. Legal Requirements: Stay up-to-date on legal requirements and regulations, including tax laws, licensing, and insurance requirements. Consult with a lawyer or accountant to ensure that your business is in compliance with all relevant laws.

22. Cost Management: Implement cost management strategies to control expenses and maximize profits. Evaluate your costs regularly, and look for ways to reduce waste and increase efficiency.

23. Route Planning: Plan your routes carefully to minimize travel time, fuel costs, and other expenses. Consider factors like road conditions, traffic patterns, and delivery schedules.

24. Freight Brokering: Consider becoming a freight broker to expand your business and generate additional revenue. Freight brokers match shippers with carriers to transport their goods, and earn a fee for their services.

25. Diversification: Diversify your services and offerings to reduce your risk and increase your revenue. Consider options like intermodal transportation, warehousing, and logistics services.

26. Partnership and Collaboration: Seek out partnership and collaboration opportunities with other trucking companies and suppliers. Collaborate on projects and initiatives to expand your network and increase your reach.

27. Innovation: Stay innovative and open to new technologies, techniques, and strategies to remain competitive in the trucking industry. Embrace change and be willing to adapt to new challenges and opportunities.

28. Market Research: Conduct market research to understand the needs of your target customers and the demands of the trucking industry. Stay informed of industry trends and developments to remain competitive.

30. Marketing: Develop a marketing strategy to promote your trucking business and attract new customers. Utilize various marketing channels, including social media, email, and advertising, to reach your target audience.

31. Sales: Develop a sales strategy to increase your revenue and grow your customer base. Offer competitive pricing, high-quality services, and strong customer relationships to win business.

32. Employee Management: Develop an employee management plan to attract and retain quality employees. Offer competitive compensation packages, benefits, and training opportunities to keep your employees motivated and engaged.

33. Time Management: Implement time management strategies to improve efficiency and productivity. Prioritize your tasks and delegate responsibilities to maximize your time and energy.

34. Financial Planning: Develop a comprehensive financial plan to manage your cash flow, budget, and investments. Utilize accounting and financial management software to help you track your expenses and revenue.

35. Human Resources: Establish a strong human resources program to manage your employees and ensure compliance with labor laws and regulations. Offer fair and transparent policies and procedures, and promote a positive work environment.

36. Contracts: Negotiate and draft contracts that clearly outline your services, pricing, and payment terms. Seek the advice of a lawyer or other professional to ensure that your contracts are legally binding and enforceable.

37. Compliance: Ensure that your trucking business is in compliance with all federal, state, and local regulations and laws, including environmental, safety, and labor regulations. Seek the advice of a lawyer or other professional if necessary.

38. Safety Culture: Develop a strong safety culture in your trucking business, and implement safety policies and procedures to protect your employees and customers. Conduct regular safety training and inspections, and reward employees who demonstrate a commitment to safety.

39. Emergency Planning: Develop an emergency plan to prepare for potential accidents, natural disasters, or other emergencies. Ensure that your employees know what to do in the event of an emergency, and conduct regular emergency drills and training.

40. Insurance: Invest in comprehensive insurance coverage to protect your business against potential losses, lawsuits, and damages. Shop around for the best coverage at the most competitive price, and seek the advice of an insurance broker if necessary.

41. Continuous Improvement: Continuously evaluate and improve your trucking business processes and systems. Seek feedback from employees, customers, and industry experts to identify areas for improvement, and

implement changes as necessary. By continuously striving for excellence, you can ensure that your trucking business remains competitive and successful.

It is important to remember that starting and scaling a trucking business takes time and effort, but the rewards can be substantial. Whether you are starting a trucking business from scratch or expanding an existing operation, the key to success is to have a clear vision, a solid plan, and a commitment to continuous improvement.

Take the time to research the trucking industry, your competition, and your target market, and use this information to develop a comprehensive business plan. Seek the advice of experts, including lawyers, accountants, and business consultants, to help you navigate the challenges and opportunities of starting and scaling your trucking business.

Remember to also stay up-to-date with industry trends, technology, and regulations, and be willing to adapt to changes as necessary. And most importantly, stay focused on your goals and remain dedicated to your business. With hard work, persistence, and a willingness to learn and grow, you can achieve great success in the trucking business.

We hope that this guide has provided you with valuable information and insights on how to start and scale your trucking business. Good luck on your journey to success!

Chapter 2.

Developing a Business Plan

Starting and scaling a trucking business requires careful planning and preparation. A business plan is a roadmap for your business that outlines your goals, strategies, and plans for success. In this chapter, we will provide you with tips and advice on how to develop a comprehensive business plan for your trucking business.

Why You Need a Business Plan

A business plan is a critical component of starting and scaling your trucking business. It provides you with a clear direction and helps you stay focused on your goals. A business plan can also be a useful tool when seeking financing or investment, as it demonstrates your commitment to your business and shows potential investors that you have a well-thought-out plan for success.

Elements of a Business Plan

A typical business plan includes the following key elements:

1. Executive Summary: A brief overview of your business, including your mission statement, target market, competition, and plans for growth.

2. Market Analysis: A thorough analysis of the trucking industry and your target market, including trends, opportunities, and challenges.

3. Competitive Analysis: An evaluation of your competition, including their strengths, weaknesses, and opportunities for differentiation.

4. Marketing Plan: A detailed description of your marketing strategies and plans for promoting your trucking business.

5. Operations Plan: A description of your operations, including your processes, systems, and facilities.

6. Financial Plan: A comprehensive analysis of your finances, including your revenue, expenses, and cash flow projections.

7. Management Team: An overview of your management team and their roles and responsibilities.

8. Implementation Plan: A timeline for implementing your business plan, including your key milestones and goals.

9. Appendices: Additional information that supports your business plan, including market research, financial projections, and other relevant data.

Tips for Developing a Business Plan

1. Research and Prepare: Research the trucking industry, your target market, and your competition to gather information and insights for your business plan. Be prepared to invest time and energy into the development of your business plan, as it will be a key tool in your success.

2. Keep it Simple: A business plan should be clear, concise, and easy to understand. Avoid using technical jargon or overly complicated language, and focus on the key elements of your business plan.

3. Be Realistic: Your business plan should be realistic and achievable, based on your resources, expertise, and market conditions. Be mindful of your limitations, and set achievable goals and milestones for your business.

4. Update Regularly: A business plan is not a one-time document, but should be reviewed and updated regularly as your business evolves and grows. Be prepared to make changes and adjustments as necessary.

5. Seek Feedback: Seek feedback from industry experts, advisors, and potential investors on your business plan. Their insights and perspectives can help you refine and improve your plan, and increase your chances of success.

Conclusion

A business plan is a critical component of starting and scaling your trucking business. It provides you with a roadmap for success and helps you stay focused on your goals. By investing time and energy into developing a comprehensive and realistic business plan, you can increase your chances of success and achieve your goals for your trucking business.

Chapter 3.

Financing Your Trucking Business

Securing financing is a crucial step in starting and scaling your trucking business. Whether you are starting a new business or expanding an existing operation, you will need access to capital to purchase trucks, hire employees, and cover operating expenses. In this chapter, we will provide you with tips and advice on how to finance your trucking business.

Sources of Financing

There are several options for financing your trucking business, including:

1. Personal Savings: You can use your personal savings to fund your trucking business, either in whole or in part. This can be a good option if you have a significant amount of savings and prefer to retain control over your business.

2. Bank Loans: You can apply for a loan from a bank or other financial institution to finance your trucking business. This option typically requires a good credit score and a well-prepared business plan.

3. Equipment Financing: You can finance the purchase of trucks and other equipment through an equipment financing loan. This option is typically used to purchase large assets such as vehicles and can be an attractive option for trucking businesses.

4. Venture Capital: If your trucking business has high growth potential, you may be able to secure financing from venture capitalists. This option typically involves giving up a portion of ownership in your business in exchange for capital.

5. Government Grants: You may be eligible for government grants to finance your trucking business, depending on your location and the type of business you operate.

Factors to Consider When Choosing a Source of Financing

When choosing a source of financing for your trucking business, there are several factors to consider, including:

1. Cost: The cost of financing can vary depending on the source, so be sure to compare the costs of different options before making a decision.

2. Repayment Terms: The repayment terms of a loan or other financing option can have a significant impact on your business, so be sure to carefully review the terms and conditions of each option before making a decision.

3. Control: Some sources of financing, such as venture capital, may involve giving up a portion of control over your business. Consider the impact this will have on your business and your long-term goals.

4. Purpose: Consider the specific use of the funds and choose a financing option that best meets your needs. For example, if you are financing the purchase of trucks,

equipment financing may be a better option than a traditional bank loan.

5. Time to Fund: The time it takes to secure financing can vary depending on the source, so be sure to consider the timeline for each option and plan accordingly.

Tips for Securing Financing

1. Prepare a Business Plan: A comprehensive and well-prepared business plan is a critical component of securing financing for your trucking business. Take the time to research and prepare a detailed plan that outlines your goals, strategies, and plans for success.

2. Build a Strong Credit Profile: A good credit score can make it easier to secure financing for your trucking business. Take steps to build a strong credit profile by paying bills on time, managing debt wisely, and avoiding credit issues.

3. Network: Networking with industry experts, lenders, and other business owners can help you identify potential sources of financing for your trucking business. Attend industry events, join business organizations, and seek out opportunities to meet with potential lenders.

4. Shop Around: Don't limit yourself to one source of financing. Shop around and compare the costs, repayment terms, and other factors of different options to find the best fit for your trucking business.

5. Negotiate: Once you have identified potential sources of financing, don't be afraid to negotiate the terms and

conditions. Work with your lender to find a financing option that meets your needs and is affordable for your business.

6. Provide Collateral: If you have assets, such as real estate or vehicles, you can use them as collateral to secure financing for your trucking business. This can help you secure a loan with more favorable terms and lower interest rates.

7. Consider Alternative Financing Options: In addition to traditional sources of financing, there are alternative options available, such as crowdfunding and peer-to-peer lending. Consider exploring these options to see if they may be a good fit for your trucking business.

Conclusion

Securing financing is a critical step in starting and scaling your trucking business. Whether you are starting a new business or expanding an existing operation, you will need access to capital to purchase trucks, hire employees, and cover operating expenses. Consider all of your options and choose a financing option that meets your needs and is affordable for your business. Don't be afraid to shop around, negotiate, and consider alternative financing options to find the best fit for your trucking business.

Chapter 4.

Choosing the Right Vehicles and Equipment for Your Business

When starting a trucking business, one of the most important decisions you will make is choosing the right vehicles and equipment. The right vehicles and equipment will help you meet the demands of your customers, increase your efficiency, and maximize your profits. In this chapter, we will explore some of the factors to consider when choosing the right vehicles and equipment for your trucking business.

1. Determine Your Needs: The first step in choosing the right vehicles and equipment for your business is to determine your needs. Consider the type of goods you will be transporting, the routes you will be driving, and the size of your operation. This will help you determine the type and size of vehicles you need to purchase.

2. Research and Compare: Once you have determined your needs, it's time to research and compare different types of vehicles and equipment. Look at the features and specifications of each option, and consider factors such as fuel efficiency, reliability, and cost. This will help you choose the right vehicles and equipment for your trucking business.

3. Consider Your Budget: When choosing vehicles and equipment, it's important to consider your budget. While it may be tempting to purchase the latest and greatest vehicles and equipment, it's important to stay within your budget. Choose vehicles and equipment

that meet your needs and are affordable for your business.

4. Think About Maintenance: Vehicles and equipment require regular maintenance to keep them in good working order. When choosing vehicles and equipment, consider the cost of maintenance and repairs. Choose vehicles and equipment that are known for their reliability and have a good reputation for low maintenance costs.

5. Leasing vs. Buying: When choosing vehicles and equipment, you have the option of leasing or buying. Leasing allows you to have access to vehicles and equipment without the upfront costs of buying. However, you will typically pay more in the long run as you are paying for the use of the vehicles and equipment. Buying allows you to own the vehicles and equipment outright, but requires a large upfront investment. Consider your financial situation and goals when choosing between leasing and buying.

6. Safety Features: Safety should be a top priority when choosing vehicles and equipment for your trucking business. Look for vehicles and equipment with features such as airbags, anti-lock brakes, and stability control. These features can help keep you and your drivers safe on the road.

Conclusion

Choosing the right vehicles and equipment is a critical step in starting and scaling your trucking business. Determine your needs, research and compare different options, consider your budget, think about maintenance, and choose vehicles and equipment that are safe and reliable. Whether you choose to lease or buy, make sure you choose vehicles and equipment that will help you meet the demands of your customers, increase your efficiency, and maximize your profits.

Chapter 5.

Establishing Operations and Logistics

Establishing operations and logistics is an important step in starting and scaling your trucking business. Having a solid operations and logistics plan in place will help you meet the demands of your customers, increase efficiency, and maximize profits. In this chapter, we will explore some of the key considerations when establishing operations and logistics for your trucking business.

1. Define Your Routes: One of the first steps in establishing operations and logistics is to define your routes. Consider the type of goods you will be transporting, the destinations you will be delivering to, and the size of your operation. This will help you determine the best routes for your trucks to take and ensure that you are maximizing efficiency.

2. Develop a Scheduling System: Developing a scheduling system is an important part of establishing operations and logistics. A good scheduling system will help you manage your fleet and ensure that your trucks are on the road and delivering goods when they are needed. Consider using software or a mobile app to help you manage your scheduling system.

3. Establish a Dispatch System: In addition to a scheduling system, you will also need to establish a dispatch system. A dispatch system is used to manage the movement of your trucks and ensure that they are on the right routes and arriving at destinations on time.

Consider using software or a mobile app to help you manage your dispatch system.

4. Plan for Maintenance: Regular maintenance is an important part of establishing operations and logistics. Develop a maintenance plan that outlines when each vehicle will be serviced, what maintenance will be performed, and how much it will cost. This will help you ensure that your vehicles are in good working order and reduce the risk of breakdowns and unplanned downtime.

5. Plan for Loading and Unloading: Loading and unloading is a critical part of the trucking business. Develop a plan for loading and unloading goods that is efficient, safe, and cost-effective. Consider using equipment such as conveyor systems and pallet jacks to help streamline the process.

6. Consider Technology: Technology is playing an increasingly important role in the trucking industry. Consider using technology to help you manage your operations and logistics, such as GPS tracking, electronic logging devices, and mobile apps. These tools can help you improve efficiency, reduce costs, and provide better customer service.

Conclusion

Establishing operations and logistics is an important step in starting and scaling your trucking business. Consider factors such as defining your routes, developing a scheduling system, establishing a dispatch system, planning for maintenance, planning for loading and unloading, and using technology. By having a solid operations and logistics plan in place, you can meet the demands of your customers, increase efficiency, and maximize profits.

Chapter 6.

Building a Strong Team

Building a strong team is one of the most important things you can do for your trucking business. Your team will be the backbone of your operation and will play a critical role in helping you achieve your goals. In this chapter, we will explore some of the key steps in building a strong team for your trucking business.

1. Hire the Right People: When hiring for your trucking business, it is important to hire the right people. Look for individuals who have experience in the trucking industry, a good driving record, and a positive attitude. Consider conducting background checks and asking for references to help ensure that you are hiring the best people for the job.

2. Offer Training and Development Opportunities: Providing training and development opportunities for your team members is an important part of building a strong team. Consider offering on-the-job training, as well as training in areas such as safety, customer service, and sales. This will help your team members grow and develop professionally, and will also help your business succeed.

3. Encourage Communication and Collaboration: Encouraging communication and collaboration is an important part of building a strong team. Make sure that your team members have the tools and resources they need to communicate effectively with each other and with customers. This will help ensure that everyone

is on the same page and working together towards a common goal.

4. Foster a Positive Work Culture: Fostering a positive work culture is another important part of building a strong team. This includes creating a workplace that is safe, respectful, and inclusive, as well as encouraging teamwork and recognizing the contributions of individual team members. When your team feels valued and supported, they will be more motivated and productive.

5. Provide Opportunities for Growth and Advancement: Providing opportunities for growth and advancement is an important part of building a strong team. Consider offering promotions, cross-training, and other opportunities for career development. This will help keep your team members engaged and motivated, and will also help ensure that your business has the talent it needs to grow and succeed.

6. Offer Competitive Compensation and Benefits: Offering competitive compensation and benefits is an important part of building a strong team. Consider offering a competitive salary, as well as benefits such as health insurance, retirement plans, and paid time off. This will help attract and retain the best talent, and will also help keep your team members motivated and engaged.

Conclusion

Building a strong team is one of the most important things you can do for your trucking business. Consider hiring the right people, offering training and development opportunities, encouraging communication and collaboration, fostering a positive work culture, providing opportunities for growth and advancement, and offering competitive compensation and benefits. By investing in your team, you can help ensure the success of your business and achieve your goals.

Chapter 7.

Marketing Your Trucking Business

Marketing is an important part of building and growing your trucking business. Your marketing efforts can help you reach new customers, build your brand, and increase your profits. In this chapter, we will explore some of the key steps in marketing your trucking business.

1. Develop a Marketing Plan: Developing a marketing plan is the first step in marketing your trucking business. Your marketing plan should include your target audience, your marketing goals, and your budget. It should also include a timeline and a plan for measuring the success of your marketing efforts.

2. Build Your Brand: Building your brand is an important part of marketing your trucking business. Your brand should reflect the values and mission of your business, and should be consistent across all of your marketing materials. Consider developing a logo, a tagline, and other visual elements that will help you stand out from your competition.

3. Utilize Online Marketing: Utilizing online marketing is an important part of marketing your trucking business. This includes building a website, using social media, and optimizing your website for search engines. Your website should include information about your business, your services, and your contact information. Your social media presence should be used to engage with customers and promote your business.

4. Utilize Direct Mail and Email Marketing: Utilizing direct mail and email marketing is another way to reach potential customers. Consider sending postcards, flyers, or emails to promote your business and to introduce your services. This can be an effective way to reach new customers and build relationships with existing customers.

5. Attend Trade Shows and Networking Events: Attending trade shows and networking events is another way to reach potential customers and promote your business. Consider exhibiting at trucking industry events, as well as attending local business events. This can be an opportunity to network with other business owners, build relationships, and find new customers.

6. Offer Special Promotions and Discounts: Offering special promotions and discounts is another way to reach new customers and promote your business. Consider offering discounts for first-time customers, as well as seasonal promotions. This can help attract new customers and encourage existing customers to use your services more frequently.

7. Use Referral Marketing: Using referral marketing is another way to reach new customers and promote your business. Consider offering incentives for customers who refer their friends and family to your business. This can be an effective way to find new customers and build your business.

Conclusion

Marketing your trucking business is an important part of building and growing your business. Consider developing a marketing plan, building your brand, utilizing online marketing, utilizing direct mail and email marketing, attending trade shows and networking events, offering special promotions and discounts, and using referral marketing. By investing in your marketing efforts, you can help reach new customers, build your brand, and increase your profits.

Chapter 8.

Navigating Regulatory Requirements

Regulatory requirements play a significant role in the trucking industry. It is important to understand the regulations that apply to your business in order to operate legally and avoid penalties and fines. In this chapter, we will explore some of the key regulatory requirements you need to be aware of as you start and grow your trucking business.

1. Federal Motor Carrier Safety Administration (FMCSA): The FMCSA is the primary federal agency responsible for regulating the trucking industry. As a trucking business owner, you will be required to register your business with the FMCSA, and you will be subject to safety and compliance regulations. Some of these regulations include hours of service rules, drug and alcohol testing requirements, and vehicle maintenance and inspection standards.

2. Department of Transportation (DOT) Number: In order to operate a commercial motor vehicle, you will need to obtain a DOT number from the FMCSA. Your DOT number is a unique identifier that is assigned to your business, and it is required on all commercial motor vehicles that you operate.

3. International Fuel Tax Agreement (IFTA): If you plan to operate your trucking business across state lines, you will need to obtain an IFTA license. This license will allow you to report and pay fuel taxes in multiple states.

4. Hazardous Materials Regulations: If you plan to transport hazardous materials, you will need to comply with regulations established by the FMCSA and the Department of Transportation (DOT). These regulations specify the types of hazardous materials that can be transported, and they outline the requirements for packaging, labeling, and documentation.

5. Electronic Logging Devices (ELDs): The FMCSA requires that all commercial motor vehicles be equipped with electronic logging devices (ELDs). ELDs are used to track and monitor hours of service, and they are designed to ensure that truck drivers comply with hours of service regulations.

6. State Regulations: In addition to federal regulations, you will also need to be aware of state regulations. State regulations can vary, but they can include licensing and permitting requirements, weight and size restrictions, and fuel tax requirements.

7. Insurance Requirements: Insurance requirements are another important aspect of regulatory compliance. You will need to obtain insurance for your trucking business, including liability insurance and cargo insurance. Your insurance coverage should be reviewed and updated regularly to ensure that you have the appropriate coverage for your business.

Conclusion

Regulatory requirements play a significant role in the trucking industry, and it is important to understand the regulations that apply to your business. Consider registering with the FMCSA, obtaining a DOT number, obtaining an IFTA license, complying with hazardous materials regulations, installing ELDs, being aware of state regulations, and obtaining insurance coverage. By understanding and complying with regulatory requirements, you can operate your trucking business legally and avoid penalties and fines.

Chapter 9.

Protecting Your Business

Starting and growing a trucking business involves a significant investment of time, money, and effort. In order to protect your investment and ensure the success of your business, it is important to take steps to protect your business from potential risks and challenges. In this chapter, we will explore some of the key ways you can protect your business and keep it on a path to success.

1. Protecting Your Vehicles and Equipment: Your vehicles and equipment are essential to the success of your trucking business, and it is important to take steps to protect them. Consider installing security systems on your vehicles, such as GPS tracking and theft prevention systems. Regular maintenance and inspections can also help to keep your vehicles and equipment in good condition and reduce the risk of breakdowns and other issues.

2. Protecting Your Business from Liabilities: Liabilities can be a significant risk for trucking businesses, particularly when it comes to accidents and other incidents involving your vehicles. To protect your business from potential liabilities, consider obtaining liability insurance, as well as insurance for your cargo and your vehicles. It is also important to have clear policies and procedures in place for your drivers, including guidelines for safe driving and accident reporting.

3. Protecting Your Business from Cyber Threats: Cyber threats are an increasing risk for businesses of all types,

and trucking businesses are no exception. In order to protect your business from cyber threats, consider implementing strong cybersecurity measures, such as firewalls, antivirus software, and encryption. You should also educate your employees about cyber threats and best practices for protecting sensitive information.

4. Protecting Your Business from Economic Downturns: Economic downturns can have a significant impact on trucking businesses, particularly if your business is heavily dependent on one industry or a specific region. In order to protect your business from economic downturns, consider diversifying your customer base and exploring new markets. It is also important to have a solid financial plan in place, including a contingency plan for economic downturns.

5. Protecting Your Business from Competition: Competition can be intense in the trucking industry, and it is important to take steps to protect your business from potential competition. Consider differentiating your business by offering unique services or by focusing on a specific niche. It is also important to stay up-to-date on industry trends and to continuously improve your operations and processes.

Conclusion

Protecting your trucking business is essential for its success and longevity. Consider protecting your vehicles and equipment, protecting your business from liabilities, protecting your business from cyber threats, protecting your business from economic downturns, and protecting your business from competition. By taking these steps, you can ensure the success and stability of your trucking business for years to come.

Chapter 10.

Building Strong Customer Relationships

In the trucking industry, building strong relationships with your customers is crucial to the success of your business. Your customers are the lifeblood of your business, and it is important to take steps to build and maintain strong relationships with them. In this chapter, we will explore some of the key strategies for building strong customer relationships in the trucking industry.

1. Providing Exceptional Service: Providing exceptional service is one of the most important factors in building strong customer relationships. This means going above and beyond to meet your customers' needs and expectations, delivering shipments on time and in good condition, and responding promptly to customer inquiries and concerns. It is also important to be flexible and accommodating, and to be willing to make adjustments or accommodate special requests when necessary.

2. Building Trust: Trust is a crucial component of any strong relationship, and it is especially important in the trucking industry. Building trust with your customers means being reliable and dependable, delivering shipments on time, and providing clear and accurate information about your services. It is also important to be transparent about your pricing and to avoid any hidden fees or charges that could erode your customers' trust.

3. Maintaining Open Communication: Maintaining open communication with your customers is another key component of building strong relationships. This means being responsive and accessible, and being willing to listen to your customers' feedback and concerns. It is also important to be proactive in your communication, keeping your customers informed about any changes or updates that may affect their shipments.

4. Building Relationships with Suppliers: Building strong relationships with your suppliers is another important aspect of building strong customer relationships. By working closely with your suppliers, you can ensure a steady supply of the goods and materials you need to meet your customers' needs. This can also help you to negotiate better pricing and reduce your costs, which can benefit both you and your customers.

5. Building Strong Community Ties: Building strong relationships with the communities where you operate is another important aspect of building strong customer relationships. This can involve participating in local events and organizations, supporting local charities and causes, and engaging in other activities that help to build your business's reputation and create positive relationships with your customers.

Conclusion

Building strong customer relationships is essential for the success of your trucking business. By providing exceptional service, building trust, maintaining open communication, building relationships with suppliers, and building strong community ties, you can create strong, long-lasting relationships with your customers that will benefit your business for years to come.

Chapter 11.

Optimizing Your Route Planning and Scheduling

Route planning and scheduling are crucial elements of any trucking business, as they help to ensure that shipments are delivered on time, within budget, and with minimal downtime. In this chapter, we will explore some strategies for optimizing your route planning and scheduling to help you achieve greater efficiency, lower costs, and stronger customer satisfaction.

1. Utilizing Technology: One of the most effective ways to optimize your route planning and scheduling is to utilize technology. There are many software programs and apps available that can help you plan routes, schedule shipments, and track delivery times and costs. These tools can help you to identify the most efficient routes, reduce downtime, and improve communication with your customers.

2. Planning Ahead: Another important strategy for optimizing your route planning and scheduling is to plan ahead. This means considering all of the factors that may impact your shipments, such as weather conditions, traffic patterns, and delivery times, and making adjustments accordingly. By anticipating potential challenges and planning ahead, you can ensure that your shipments are delivered on time and with minimal disruptions.

3. Optimizing Loads: Optimizing your loads is another important aspect of route planning and scheduling. This means ensuring that your vehicles are loaded to their maximum capacity, reducing the number of trips required to deliver a shipment and minimizing the amount of time and fuel required. It is also important to consider the weight and size of your shipments, as well as any special requirements, to ensure that your loads are optimized and your vehicles are used to their full potential.

4. Collaborating with Customers: Collaborating with your customers is another important strategy for optimizing your route planning and scheduling. This means working closely with your customers to understand their needs and preferences, and making adjustments to your schedules and routes accordingly. By collaborating with your customers, you can ensure that your shipments are delivered on time and with minimal disruptions, and you can also build stronger, more positive relationships with your customers.

5. Continuously Monitoring and Improving: Finally, it is important to continuously monitor and improve your route planning and scheduling to ensure that you are achieving the best possible results. This means regularly reviewing your delivery times, costs, and customer satisfaction, and making adjustments as needed. It is also important to seek out feedback from your customers and employees, and to be open to new ideas and strategies for optimizing your route planning and scheduling.

Conclusion

Optimizing your route planning and scheduling is crucial for the success of your trucking business. By utilizing technology, planning ahead, optimizing loads, collaborating with customers, and continuously monitoring and improving, you can ensure that your shipments are delivered on time, within budget, and with minimal downtime. By taking these steps, you can improve your efficiency, reduce your costs, and build stronger relationships with your customers.

Chapter 12.

Maximizing Load Capacity and Utilization

Maximizing load capacity and utilization is essential for maximizing the efficiency and profitability of your trucking business. By utilizing your vehicles and equipment to their full potential, you can reduce your costs, improve your delivery times, and ensure that your business runs smoothly and efficiently. In this chapter, we will explore some strategies for maximizing load capacity and utilization in your trucking business.

1. Understanding Your Fleet: One of the first steps in maximizing load capacity and utilization is to understand your fleet. This means knowing the size and weight of your vehicles, as well as their load capacity and the types of loads they can carry. By understanding your fleet, you can make informed decisions about which vehicles and equipment to use for each shipment, ensuring that your loads are optimized and your vehicles are used to their full potential.

2. Utilizing Trailers and Containers: Utilizing trailers and containers is another important strategy for maximizing load capacity and utilization. By using trailers and containers, you can transport larger and heavier loads, reducing the number of trips required to deliver a shipment and minimizing the amount of time and fuel required. It is also important to consider the type of trailer or container you use, as some may be better suited for specific types of loads, such as refrigerated goods or hazardous materials.

3. Loading Smarter: Loading your vehicles smarter is another key strategy for maximizing load capacity and utilization. This means ensuring that your vehicles are loaded to their maximum capacity, while also taking into account the weight distribution and stability of your loads. By loading your vehicles smarter, you can improve your delivery times, reduce your costs, and minimize the risk of damage or injury to your drivers.
4. Optimizing Delivery Schedules: Optimizing your delivery schedules is another important aspect of maximizing load capacity and utilization. This means scheduling deliveries in a way that minimizes downtime and maximizes the efficiency of your routes. For example, you may choose to make multiple deliveries to one location, or you may schedule deliveries to coincide with other shipments, reducing the number of trips required and improving your delivery times.
5. Collaborating with Customers: Collaborating with your customers is another key strategy for maximizing load capacity and utilization. By working closely with your customers, you can understand their needs and preferences, and make adjustments to your delivery schedules and routes accordingly. By collaborating with your customers, you can ensure that your loads are optimized, your delivery times are improved, and you build stronger relationships with your customers.

Conclusion

Maximizing load capacity and utilization is crucial for the success of your trucking business. By utilizing your vehicles and equipment to their full potential, reducing your costs, and improving your delivery times, you can ensure that your business runs smoothly and efficiently. By following the strategies outlined in this chapter, including understanding your fleet, utilizing trailers and containers, loading smarter, optimizing delivery schedules, and collaborating with your customers, you can maximize your load capacity and utilization, and achieve greater success in your trucking business.

Chapter 13.

Implementing Technology Solutions

In today's rapidly evolving business landscape, technology is playing an increasingly important role in the trucking industry. From optimizing routes and schedules to improving communication with customers and drivers, technology has the power to transform the way you do business. In this chapter, we will explore some of the technology solutions available to trucking businesses, and how you can use these solutions to improve your operations and grow your business.

1. Route Planning and Optimization Software: Route planning and optimization software can help you to plan and execute efficient and cost-effective routes, saving you time and fuel costs. These solutions use data such as traffic patterns, weather conditions, and road conditions to create optimized routes, and can even suggest alternative routes in real-time if conditions change.

2. Electronic Logging Devices (ELDs): Electronic logging devices (ELDs) are a critical technology solution for trucking businesses, as they help you to comply with federal regulations regarding hours of service (HOS) for drivers. ELDs automatically track and record a driver's HOS, ensuring that your drivers stay within the legal limits and that you remain compliant with federal regulations.

3. GPS Tracking: GPS tracking can help you to monitor the location and status of your vehicles and drivers in real-time, allowing you to optimize your delivery schedules

and respond quickly to any unexpected changes. This technology can also help you to reduce fuel costs by monitoring idling and speeding, and can provide valuable data to help you make informed decisions about your operations.

4. Communication and Dispatch Tools: Communication and dispatch tools can help you to improve communication with your drivers and customers, and streamline your dispatch operations. With these tools, you can send messages and updates to your drivers in real-time, and receive updates on delivery status, vehicle location, and more.

5. Fleet Maintenance Software: Fleet maintenance software can help you to manage and track your vehicle maintenance, reducing downtime and ensuring that your vehicles are always in top condition. This software can track maintenance schedules, notify you of upcoming services, and store maintenance records, making it easy for you to keep your vehicles in top condition.

6. Mobile Apps: Mobile apps can help you to manage your trucking business from anywhere, at any time. With these apps, you can access real-time data and updates, communicate with drivers and customers, and manage your operations with ease. Whether you're on the road or in the office, mobile apps can help you to stay connected and in control of your trucking business.

Conclusion

Technology has the power to transform the trucking industry, and implementing technology solutions can help you to improve your operations, reduce costs, and grow your business. By using solutions such as route planning and optimization software, electronic logging devices, GPS tracking, communication and dispatch tools, fleet maintenance software, and mobile apps, you can streamline your operations, enhance your customer service, and achieve greater success in your trucking business. It's important to keep in mind that technology solutions are constantly evolving, and that it is important to stay up to date on the latest innovations and trends in the trucking industry. By embracing technology and staying ahead of the curve, you can ensure that your trucking business remains competitive and successful for years to come.

Chapter 14.

Handling Disputes and Resolving Conflicts

Running a trucking business can be a complex and challenging endeavor, and at times, disputes and conflicts are inevitable. It's important to have strategies in place to handle these situations effectively and efficiently, as they can have a significant impact on your business operations, reputation, and bottom line. In this chapter, we'll take a closer look at how to handle disputes and resolve conflicts in the trucking business.

First and foremost, it's important to have a clear understanding of the different types of disputes and conflicts that can arise in the trucking business. These can include disagreements with customers, disputes with carriers or other business partners, and conflicts with employees. It's essential to be prepared for these situations and to have processes in place for resolving them quickly and fairly.

One of the key elements of resolving disputes and conflicts is effective communication. In many cases, misunderstandings and disagreements can be quickly and easily resolved through clear and direct communication between all parties involved. Encourage your employees and business partners to communicate openly and honestly, and always seek to find common ground and understand each other's perspectives.

It's also important to have a formal dispute resolution process in place, such as mediation or arbitration. This can help to ensure that disputes are handled in a fair and impartial manner, and can prevent minor disagreements from escalating into larger, more serious problems. In some cases, it may also be necessary to involve legal counsel to help resolve disputes.

Another effective strategy for resolving disputes and conflicts is to involve a neutral third-party, such as a mediator or arbitrator. These individuals are trained to facilitate communication between parties and to help resolve disputes in a fair and impartial manner. By involving a neutral third-party, you can reduce the risk of misunderstandings and prevent minor disagreements from escalating into larger, more serious problems.

In addition, it's important to have clear and concise policies and procedures in place that outline how disputes and conflicts should be handled. This can include guidelines for communication, as well as steps for resolving disputes and conflicts through mediation, arbitration, or legal action. Having these policies in place can help to ensure that disputes are handled consistently and fairly, and can prevent misunderstandings and disagreements from escalating into larger problems.

Finally, it's essential to maintain a positive and professional attitude throughout the dispute resolution process. This can help to maintain good relationships with your customers, employees, and business partners, and can prevent disputes and conflicts from having a negative impact on your business operations and reputation.

In conclusion, handling disputes and resolving conflicts is an important aspect of running a successful trucking business. By being prepared, communicating effectively, and having clear policies and procedures in place, you can effectively manage disputes and conflicts, and maintain a positive and productive business environment.

Chapter 15.

Expanding Your Fleet

Congratulations! If you've made it this far, it means that your trucking business is thriving and you're ready for growth. Expanding your fleet is an exciting next step, and it's important to approach it carefully to ensure success.

Here are some tips for making the transition to a larger fleet.

1. Assess Your Needs: Before you start buying new trucks, it's important to assess your current and future needs. Consider the types of loads you're transporting, the size of your customer base, and the routes you're driving. This will help you determine the types of vehicles and the number of vehicles you'll need to expand your fleet.

2. Evaluate Your Finances: Expanding your fleet is a significant investment, so it's important to make sure you have the financial resources to support it. This might mean taking out a loan, seeking investment, or dipping into savings. Make sure you have a solid plan in place to cover the costs of buying new trucks, maintaining them, and hiring new drivers.

3. Consider Your Workforce: As you expand your fleet, you'll need to hire more drivers. Make sure you have a solid plan in place for attracting and retaining top talent. Offer competitive salaries, benefits, and opportunities for growth. Additionally, make sure your

current employees are happy and engaged, as they can play a key role in recruiting new drivers.

4. Choose the Right Vehicles: When it comes to buying new trucks, it's important to choose the right vehicles for your business. Consider the types of loads you're transporting, the size of your customer base, and the routes you're driving. Make sure the vehicles you buy are fuel efficient, reliable, and capable of handling the demands of your business.

5. Develop a Maintenance Plan: Expanding your fleet means you'll have more trucks to maintain, so it's important to have a solid plan in place for keeping them in top condition. This might include regular maintenance check-ups, keeping spare parts on hand, and having a dedicated maintenance team in place.

6. Monitor Your Fleet: As you expand your fleet, it's important to monitor its performance and make sure everything is running smoothly. This might include tracking fuel consumption, vehicle maintenance, and driver performance. Use this information to make informed decisions about how to optimize your fleet and improve your bottom line.

Expanding your fleet is a significant step in the growth of your trucking business, and it's important to approach it carefully. By assessing your needs, evaluating your finances, considering your workforce, choosing the right vehicles, developing a maintenance plan, and monitoring your fleet, you can ensure that your expansion is a success. Good luck!

Chapter 16.

Navigating the Freight Market

The freight market is one of the most important components of the trucking industry, and it's essential to understand it if you want to build a successful trucking business. The freight market refers to the buying and selling of goods and commodities between producers, distributors, and consumers. To be successful in the freight market, you need to have a good understanding of the different types of freight, the supply and demand dynamics, and the pricing models that are used.

One of the key things to understand about the freight market is that it's constantly changing. The demand for different goods and services changes based on a variety of factors, including economic conditions, seasonality, and consumer trends. As a result, it's important to be flexible and able to adapt to changes in the market.

To navigate the freight market, it's important to do your research. This includes keeping up to date with industry news, following market trends, and using market data to make informed decisions. You can use websites like FreightWaves, JOC, and Freightos to access real-time market data and analysis. You can also join industry groups and attend trade shows to network with other trucking professionals and get a better understanding of the market.

Another key aspect of navigating the freight market is choosing the right freight to haul. This includes considering factors such as the type of cargo, the destination, and the level of demand. You can use tools like load boards to find available freight, but it's important to be cautious about the loads you accept. Make sure to thoroughly research the shipper and the route before accepting a load, and always verify that the cargo is properly insured.

Once you've chosen the right freight to haul, it's time to negotiate the price. Pricing in the freight market is based on a variety of factors, including the type of cargo, the distance traveled, and the level of demand. You can use tools like Freightos or DAT to get an idea of current market rates, but it's important to keep in mind that rates can change quickly, so you need to be prepared to adjust your pricing as needed.

Finally, it's important to have a good relationship with your customers and to be able to communicate effectively with them. This includes being transparent about your prices, explaining the value that you bring to the table, and being responsive to their needs and concerns. Building strong customer relationships is essential to success in the freight market, and it's something that requires time, effort, and commitment.

In conclusion, navigating the freight market is a critical component of building a successful trucking business. To be successful, you need to be informed, flexible, and proactive. You need to understand the market, choose the right freight to haul, negotiate the right price, and build strong customer relationships. With the right approach, you can thrive in the freight market and grow your trucking business to new heights.

Chapter 17.

Developing a Safety Culture

As a trucking business owner, one of your top priorities should be the safety of your drivers, other motorists, and the general public. The trucking industry has a unique set of risks and challenges, which means that safety should be a top concern. In this chapter, we'll explore how to create a safety culture within your organization, ensuring that everyone is on the same page when it comes to operating safely on the roads.

A strong safety culture starts with clear policies and procedures that outline expectations for driver behavior, maintenance of vehicles, and equipment, as well as other critical areas of operation. It's essential that you communicate these policies and procedures to your drivers and other team members, as well as ensure they understand the importance of following them. Regular training and refresher courses can help reinforce the importance of safety, and keep everyone up-to-date on the latest regulations and best practices.

In addition to having clear policies and procedures in place, you should also invest in the right equipment and technology to support safe operations. This can include things like GPS tracking systems, telematics, and advanced safety features for your vehicles. By equipping your drivers with the tools they need to operate safely, you'll help reduce the risk of accidents and incidents on the road.

Another critical aspect of developing a safety culture is regular communication with your drivers. Encourage them to speak up if they see something that could be unsafe or if they have concerns about their equipment or their route. By fostering an environment where safety is always a top priority, you'll be able to create a positive and supportive culture that helps to reduce the risk of accidents and incidents.

In addition to internal policies and procedures, you should also familiarize yourself with the regulatory requirements for the trucking industry. This includes compliance with Federal Motor Carrier Safety Administration (FMCSA) regulations, as well as state-specific requirements. By staying up-to-date on these regulations, you'll be able to ensure that your business is operating within the law and that you're meeting all of the necessary safety requirements.

Finally, it's important to recognize the value of regular safety audits and assessments. These assessments can help identify areas for improvement, and allow you to take proactive steps to reduce the risk of accidents and incidents on the road. By regularly reviewing and updating your safety policies and procedures, you'll be able to ensure that your business is always operating in the safest possible manner.

In conclusion, developing a strong safety culture within your trucking business is essential for protecting your drivers, other motorists, and the general public. By creating clear policies and procedures, investing in the right equipment and technology, fostering open communication, and staying up-to-date on regulatory requirements, you'll be well on your way to creating a safe and secure environment for everyone involved in your business.

Chapter 18.

Staying Ahead of the Competition

Starting and growing a successful trucking business takes a lot of hard work and dedication. But even the best businesses can face challenges from competitors. The trucking industry is incredibly competitive, with many companies offering similar services and prices. To stay ahead of the competition, you need to be proactive and strategic. In this chapter, we'll cover some of the best practices for staying ahead of the competition in the trucking business.

1. Know Your Competition

The first step to staying ahead of the competition is to understand who they are and what they offer. Research your competitors and get to know their strengths and weaknesses. Take a look at their websites, social media accounts, and customer reviews to learn more about their services and reputation.

2. Offer Unique Services

One way to set yourself apart from the competition is to offer unique services that they don't. For example, you could specialize in transportation for hazardous materials or offer faster delivery times. The more you can differentiate yourself from your competitors, the more likely you are to stand out in the minds of potential customers.

3. Build Strong Relationships with Customers

Building strong relationships with customers is another key to staying ahead of the competition. Offer excellent customer service and go above and beyond to meet the needs of your customers. This could include providing regular updates on the status of their shipments, offering competitive pricing, or even offering extra services like packing and unpacking.

4. Invest in Technology

Technology is playing an increasingly important role in the trucking industry. From route planning and optimization software to GPS tracking and telematics, technology can help you run your business more efficiently and effectively. Investing in technology can give you a competitive edge and help you stay ahead of the competition.

5. Stay Up-to-Date on Industry Trends

The trucking industry is constantly evolving, so it's important to stay up-to-date on the latest trends and developments. Attend industry conferences, read trade publications, and follow relevant news sources to stay informed. This can help you stay ahead of the competition and make informed decisions about your business.

6. Continuously Improve Your Operations

Finally, continuously improving your operations is key to staying ahead of the competition. Regularly review your processes and procedures and look for ways to streamline and optimize them. Consider implementing new technologies, improving your training programs, and investing in employee development to help your business stay ahead of the competition.

In conclusion, staying ahead of the competition in the trucking business requires a combination of knowledge, strategy, and continuous improvement. By understanding your competitors, offering unique services, building strong relationships with customers, investing in technology, staying up-to-date on industry trends, and continuously improving your operations, you can set yourself apart and stay ahead of the competition.

Chapter 19.

Streamlining Dispatch and Communications

Effective dispatch and communication are essential for the success of any trucking business. Poor communication can result in missed deadlines, missed deliveries, and dissatisfied customers, all of which can damage your reputation and bottom line. On the other hand, having a streamlined dispatch and communication system can help you increase efficiency, reduce downtime, and improve customer satisfaction.

There are several key components to consider when developing your dispatch and communication strategy.

These include:

1. Dispatch software: Dispatch software allows you to manage all aspects of your operations from a central location. This includes scheduling, dispatch, tracking, and invoicing. Look for software that is user-friendly and customizable, and that integrates with other systems you already use.

2. Mobile devices: Investing in mobile devices for your drivers, such as smartphones or tablets, can help you streamline communications and reduce downtime. With mobile devices, drivers can receive real-time updates on their deliveries, report issues or delays, and keep in touch with dispatchers and other drivers.

3. Two-way radios: Two-way radios are an essential tool for trucking businesses. They allow drivers to communicate with each other and with dispatch,

reducing the need for cell phone usage while driving. Make sure to invest in high-quality radios and invest in training for your drivers to ensure they know how to use them effectively.

4. Dispatch protocols: Establishing clear dispatch protocols can help you avoid confusion and ensure that everyone is on the same page. This includes guidelines for how drivers should communicate with dispatch, how deliveries should be prioritized, and how to handle unexpected issues that may arise.

5. Driver training: Providing drivers with regular training on dispatch protocols, mobile devices, and two-way radios can help ensure that everyone is using these tools effectively. Make sure to provide ongoing training and support, and be open to feedback from drivers about what works and what doesn't.

By implementing these strategies, you can improve communication and reduce downtime, which can help you increase efficiency and reduce costs. Additionally, having a streamlined dispatch and communication system can help you build stronger relationships with customers by providing them with real-time updates on their deliveries and improving response times.

One final word of advice: make sure to regularly evaluate and refine your dispatch and communication strategies. As your business grows, your needs will change, and you may need to adjust your strategies accordingly. Stay flexible and be open to new ideas and technologies that can help you improve communication and streamline your operations.

Chapter 20.

Managing Fuel Costs and Efficiency

As a trucking business owner, one of the biggest expenses you'll face is the cost of fuel. Fuel prices can be volatile and can significantly impact your bottom line, making it essential to have a solid strategy for managing fuel costs and efficiency. In this chapter, we'll explore some of the best practices for maximizing fuel efficiency and reducing costs.

One of the first things you can do to improve fuel efficiency is to maintain your vehicles. Regular maintenance helps to ensure that your trucks are running smoothly and that there are no mechanical issues that could be causing unnecessary fuel consumption. This includes regularly checking tires for proper inflation, regularly changing the air filters, and ensuring that all parts are in good working condition.

Another way to improve fuel efficiency is by optimizing your routes. This can be done by using mapping software to determine the most fuel-efficient routes, taking into account factors such as road conditions, traffic patterns, and speed limits. You can also use telematics systems to monitor your trucks in real-time and identify any opportunities for improving fuel efficiency.

Another key factor to consider when trying to reduce fuel costs is reducing idling time. Idling engines consume a significant amount of fuel, so it's important to limit the amount of time your trucks spend idling. You can do this by encouraging drivers to turn off their engines when they're not driving, or by installing automatic shutoff systems that will turn off the engine after a certain period of idling.

In addition to reducing idling time, there are other ways to reduce fuel consumption as well. For example, reducing the weight of your vehicles can help to reduce fuel consumption, as can using aerodynamic devices to reduce wind resistance. You can also reduce fuel consumption by driving at a consistent speed, rather than accelerating and decelerating frequently.

Finally, you can also save on fuel costs by purchasing fuel at the right time. By monitoring fuel prices, you can make purchases when prices are low and avoid buying fuel when prices are high. You can also take advantage of fuel discounts offered by fuel suppliers, or negotiate with fuel suppliers to secure better pricing.

In conclusion, managing fuel costs and efficiency is critical to the success of your trucking business. By using these strategies, you can significantly reduce your fuel costs, improve your bottom line, and help ensure the long-term success of your business.

Chapter 21.

Implementing Driver Incentives and Rewards

As a trucking business owner, one of your most valuable assets is your drivers. Keeping them motivated, engaged, and committed to your company is key to ensuring long-term success. One way to do this is by implementing driver incentives and rewards.

The first step in developing a driver incentives program is to identify what motivates your drivers. Some drivers may be motivated by financial incentives, while others may value things like time off, recognition, or career advancement opportunities. Take the time to get to know your drivers and find out what motivates them.

Once you have a clear understanding of what motivates your drivers, you can start developing an incentives program.

Here are a few suggestions to consider:

1. Financial incentives: Cash bonuses, extra pay for safe driving, or fuel efficiency bonuses are all effective financial incentives.
2. Time off: Offer extra time off for drivers who achieve certain milestones or have a safe driving record.
3. Recognition: Consider implementing a driver of the month program or recognizing drivers for their

achievements in a company-wide meeting or newsletter.

4. Career advancement opportunities: Invest in training and development opportunities for your drivers, or provide them with the opportunity to take on additional responsibilities within the company.

When implementing your incentives program, it's important to communicate regularly with your drivers to keep them engaged and motivated. For example, send out regular updates on how the program is going and how drivers can earn rewards. You can also provide feedback on their performance and encourage them to share any ideas they have for the program.

It's also important to keep the incentives program flexible and adaptable. Regularly review and evaluate the program to see what's working and what's not, and make changes as needed.

Incentives and rewards programs can be a powerful tool in retaining and motivating your drivers. By understanding what motivates your drivers and developing a comprehensive incentives program, you can create a positive work environment and keep your drivers committed to your company for the long haul.

Chapter 22.

Understanding Taxes and Recordkeeping

Starting and running a trucking business can be a complex and challenging task, but with the right planning and preparation, it can also be highly rewarding. One of the critical components of running a successful trucking business is understanding the various tax and recordkeeping requirements that you'll need to comply with. In this chapter, we'll provide an overview of the tax obligations you'll face as a trucking business owner and offer some tips for keeping accurate and comprehensive records.

Tax Obligations for Trucking Businesses

As a trucking business owner, you'll need to comply with a variety of tax requirements, including payroll taxes, sales taxes, and excise taxes. You'll also need to pay taxes on any profits you earn, and you'll need to keep detailed records of all of your business income and expenses to help you calculate your tax liabilities accurately.

One of the key tax obligations you'll need to comply with as a trucking business owner is payroll taxes. If you have employees, you'll need to pay taxes on their wages, including federal and state income taxes, Social Security taxes, and Medicare taxes. You'll also need to make contributions to the unemployment insurance program and to any state or local workers' compensation programs that apply.

Another important tax obligation you'll face as a trucking business owner is sales tax. Depending on the state or municipality where you operate, you may need to collect and pay sales tax on the transportation services you provide. In some cases, you may be required to register for a sales tax permit and collect sales tax on each transaction.

Excise taxes are another type of tax you'll need to be aware of as a trucking business owner. Excise taxes are taxes on specific goods or services, such as fuel taxes or highway use taxes. Depending on where you operate, you may be required to pay these taxes on a regular basis, and you'll need to keep accurate records of the amounts you've paid.

Recordkeeping for Trucking Businesses

To comply with the various tax obligations you'll face as a trucking business owner, you'll need to keep accurate and comprehensive records of all of your business income and expenses. This will help you to calculate your tax liabilities accurately, and it will also provide you with valuable information that you can use to make informed business decisions.

One of the best ways to keep track of your business income and expenses is to use a bookkeeping system, such as QuickBooks or Xero. These systems allow you to enter transactions and categorize them by type, such as expenses for fuel, supplies, and wages, and income from transportation services. You can then generate reports that provide you with a detailed overview of your business finances.

In addition to using a bookkeeping system, you should also keep detailed receipts and invoices for all of your business transactions. This will provide you with a paper trail that you can use to support your tax returns and resolve any disputes that may arise.

It's also important to keep accurate records of your vehicle expenses, including fuel, maintenance, and repairs. This information can be used to calculate the tax-deductible portion of your vehicle expenses and to help you track your fuel efficiency and costs.

Conclusion

Understanding the tax and recordkeeping requirements for your trucking business is critical to its success. By keeping accurate and comprehensive records and complying with all of the tax obligations you'll face, you can minimize the risk of tax penalties and disputes and ensure that your business remains financially healthy and sustainable.

Chapter 23.

Building Strong Relationships with Suppliers and Partners

Starting and scaling a trucking business is a challenging and complex task, and having strong relationships with suppliers and partners can make a huge difference. When you have trusted suppliers and partners, you can ensure that you have the necessary equipment, parts, and support to keep your operations running smoothly. These relationships can also help you access new opportunities, reduce costs, and increase your competitiveness in the marketplace.

Building Strong Relationships with Suppliers

One of the most important relationships you'll have as a trucking business owner is with your suppliers. You'll need a reliable source of trucks, trailers, and other equipment, as well as access to parts, maintenance services, and support. When selecting suppliers, it's important to look for companies that offer quality products and services, competitive prices, and excellent customer support. Building a relationship with these suppliers can take time and effort, but it will pay off in the long run.

Here are some tips for building strong relationships with suppliers:

1. Communicate regularly: One of the keys to building strong relationships with suppliers is to communicate regularly. Make sure you are in touch with your suppliers regularly, whether it's through email, phone

calls, or in-person visits. This will help you stay on top of any changes in the market, any new products or services that may be of interest, and any issues that may arise.

2. Be transparent: When communicating with your suppliers, be transparent about your needs and expectations. Let them know what you are looking for and how you expect to receive it. This will help to ensure that there are no misunderstandings and will help to build trust.

3. Negotiate prices: To keep costs low, it's important to negotiate prices with your suppliers. This can be a delicate process, but it's important to get the best deal possible. Be transparent about your budget and what you can afford to pay, and work with your supplier to find a mutually beneficial agreement.

4. Provide feedback: Providing feedback to your suppliers is another way to build strong relationships. When you receive good service or a quality product, be sure to let them know. This will help them improve their services and products, and will also help you get better value for your money.

Building Strong Relationships with Partners

In addition to building strong relationships with suppliers, it's also important to build strong relationships with partners. Partners can be anyone from other trucking businesses, freight brokers, or logistics companies. When you have strong relationships with partners, you can access new business opportunities, increase your competitiveness, and reduce costs.

Here are some tips for building strong relationships with partners:

1. Network: One of the keys to building strong relationships with partners is to network. Attend industry events, join trade organizations, and connect with other trucking businesses. This will help you build a network of partners and will increase your visibility in the industry.

2. Look for mutual benefits: When building relationships with partners, look for opportunities to work together to achieve mutual benefits. This could be through joint ventures, shared marketing initiatives, or shared services.

3. Communicate regularly: Regular communication is also key when building relationships with partners. Make sure you are in touch regularly and that you are keeping each other informed about any changes or developments in your businesses.

4. Build trust: Trust is essential when building relationships with partners. Make sure you are transparent about your business and that you are committed to working together for the long-term.

In conclusion, building strong relationships with suppliers and partners is an important aspect of running a successful trucking business. These relationships can help you access new business opportunities, reduce costs, and Building Strong Relationships with Suppliers and Partners

Chapter 24.

Managing Maintenance and Repairs

In the trucking industry, keeping your vehicles and equipment in top condition is crucial for the success of your business. Regular maintenance and timely repairs are necessary to ensure that your trucks are always on the road, delivering goods and earning revenue. Here are some tips for managing maintenance and repairs for your trucking business.

1. Create a maintenance schedule - Creating a regular maintenance schedule for your vehicles and equipment is important for ensuring that they receive the proper care and attention they need. This schedule should include regular check-ups, oil changes, and inspections, as well as any other necessary maintenance tasks.

2. Hire a mechanic - Consider hiring a mechanic or team of mechanics to take care of your maintenance and repairs. A professional mechanic will have the knowledge and experience to identify any potential problems early on and make necessary repairs to keep your trucks running smoothly.

3. Use technology to track maintenance and repairs - There are various software programs available that allow you to track maintenance and repairs for your vehicles and equipment. This technology can help you keep track of when maintenance is due, what has been done, and what needs to be done in the future, saving you time and effort.

4. Set aside a budget for maintenance and repairs - Regular maintenance and repairs can be costly, so it's important to set aside a budget for these expenses. This can help you to plan for these expenses and ensure that you always have the funds available when you need them.

5. Regularly inspect your vehicles and equipment - Regular inspections of your vehicles and equipment can help to identify potential problems early on and ensure that they receive the proper care and attention they need. Make sure to inspect the tires, brakes, and suspension systems, as well as any other key components of your vehicles and equipment.

6. Use preventive maintenance - Preventive maintenance is a proactive approach to maintenance that focuses on preventing problems before they occur. This can involve regular check-ups and inspections, as well as the use of high-quality products and components. By investing in preventive maintenance, you can reduce the likelihood of breakdowns and improve the overall performance of your vehicles and equipment.

7. Work with trusted suppliers and partners - Building strong relationships with trusted suppliers and partners can help you to ensure that your vehicles and equipment receive the best care and attention they need. These relationships can also help you to secure discounts and special deals on maintenance and repair services, saving you money in the long run.

In conclusion, regular maintenance and timely repairs are key to the success of your trucking business. By following these tips and taking a proactive approach to maintenance and repairs, you can keep your vehicles and equipment running smoothly and ensure that your business continues to thrive.

Chapter 25.

Improving Logistics and Supply Chain Management

Running a successful trucking business is all about efficient logistics and supply chain management. From coordinating deliveries and managing inventory to ensuring that you're utilizing your vehicles and resources to their fullest potential, there's a lot that goes into keeping your business running smoothly. In this chapter, we'll explore some strategies for improving your logistics and supply chain management so that you can take your business to the next level.

One of the most important things you can do to improve your logistics is to invest in technology solutions. There are a variety of tools and software platforms available that can help you streamline your operations and optimize your delivery routes. For example, GPS tracking software can give you real-time visibility into your vehicles' locations and help you plan your deliveries more effectively. Fleet management software can help you keep track of your vehicles' maintenance schedules, fuel consumption, and other important metrics, so that you can make more informed decisions about your operations.

Another key strategy for improving your logistics and supply chain management is to build strong relationships with your suppliers and partners. This can include things like working closely with your trucking companies to optimize your delivery schedules and negotiating favorable pricing and payment terms with your suppliers. By developing strong, trustworthy relationships with your partners, you can reduce the risk of supply chain disruptions and ensure that your business is always running smoothly.

Another important consideration is the way that you manage your inventory. Whether you're transporting goods for clients or running your own delivery routes, it's essential to have a system in place for tracking your inventory and ensuring that you have the right supplies on hand at all times. This can involve using tools like barcoding and RFID tracking, as well as maintaining accurate records of your deliveries and shipments.

Finally, it's important to stay on top of industry trends and developments in logistics and supply chain management. Whether it's new regulations, technological innovations, or emerging best practices, it's important to stay informed and stay ahead of the curve. You can do this by attending industry events and conferences, reading trade publications, and networking with other trucking professionals.

In conclusion, by investing in technology solutions, building strong relationships with suppliers and partners, managing your inventory effectively, and staying on top of industry trends, you can improve your logistics and supply chain management and take your trucking business to the next level. Whether you're just starting out or you're looking to grow your existing business, these strategies can help you achieve your goals and build a thriving trucking enterprise.

Chapter 26.

Evaluating and Negotiating Contracts

When you're starting and running a trucking business, contracts are a critical aspect of your operations. Contracts can be used to secure loads, partnerships, or even services like maintenance and repairs. But, with so many contracts to manage, it can be easy to feel overwhelmed and make mistakes. To help ensure your success, it's important to understand the basics of evaluating and negotiating contracts.

Evaluating Contracts

Before you sign on the dotted line, it's important to thoroughly evaluate the contract you're being presented with. This includes understanding the terms and conditions, as well as any potential liabilities or risks involved. To start, consider the following:

- Terms and Conditions: What are the delivery dates, payment terms, and any other specific requirements outlined in the contract? Make sure you fully understand the expectations and obligations of both parties.
- Liabilities and Risks: What kind of risks and liabilities are involved in the contract? For example, who is responsible for damages if a load is damaged during transit? Make sure you're fully aware of any potential issues and what you need to do to mitigate them.
- Legal Requirements: What are the legal requirements for the contract? Make sure the contract complies with

all relevant laws and regulations, including those specific to the trucking industry.

Negotiating Contracts

Once you've thoroughly evaluated the contract, it's time to start negotiating. This may involve working with a lawyer or other professional to help you understand the legal aspects of the contract and negotiate the best terms possible. Here are some tips to help you navigate the negotiation process:

- Know Your Goals: Before you start negotiating, take the time to determine what you want to achieve through the contract. This will help you stay focused and negotiate more effectively.
- Communicate Clearly: Communication is key when it comes to contract negotiations. Make sure you understand what the other party is looking for and what their expectations are. And, be clear and concise about your own goals and expectations.
- Be Prepared to Compromise: Contract negotiations often involve give-and-take, so be prepared to make compromises in order to reach a mutually beneficial agreement.
- Keep an Open Mind: Be open to different ideas and approaches. You may not always get exactly what you want, but by being flexible and working together, you may be able to find a solution that works for everyone.

- Get it in Writing: Finally, make sure the final agreement is put in writing and signed by both parties. This helps ensure everyone is on the same page and there are no misunderstandings.

In conclusion, evaluating and negotiating contracts is a critical aspect of running a trucking business. By taking the time to thoroughly evaluate the contract, understand your goals, communicate clearly, and be prepared to compromise, you can negotiate the best possible terms for your business.

Chapter 27.

Enhancing Customer Service

As a trucking business owner, you have the opportunity to make a real difference in the lives of your customers. Whether you are hauling goods for retailers, transporting construction materials, or delivering packages, your customers are counting on you to get their items to their destination safely and on time. That's why enhancing customer service should be a top priority in your business.

One of the best ways to improve customer service is to understand your customers' needs and preferences. This can be achieved through regular communication, surveys, and focus groups. You can also use customer feedback to identify areas where you can make improvements. For example, if you receive consistent complaints about long wait times, you might consider investing in a dispatch system that allows you to manage your drivers and shipments more efficiently.

Another important aspect of enhancing customer service is to have a dedicated team in place to handle customer inquiries and complaints. This team should be knowledgeable about your business, your products and services, and your customers' needs. They should also have the tools and resources they need to quickly and effectively resolve any issues that may arise.

To further improve customer service, you should also focus on delivering a high-quality product. This means making sure your trucks are well-maintained and equipped with the latest safety features, and that your drivers are trained and licensed to operate commercial vehicles. It also means paying attention to the packaging and handling of your shipments, to minimize the risk of damage during transit.

In addition to delivering a quality product, you should also consider offering value-added services that your customers may appreciate. For example, you might offer delivery and pickup services, storage and warehousing, or customized packaging and labeling. These services can help you stand out from your competition and attract new customers.

Finally, it's important to be responsive and flexible in your approach to customer service. This means being available to your customers when they need you, and being willing to make changes and accommodate their needs. For example, if a customer needs to make an urgent shipment, you should be willing to accommodate their request and make arrangements to get the shipment to its destination on time.

In conclusion, enhancing customer service is essential for the success of your trucking business. By understanding your customers' needs, delivering a high-quality product, offering value-added services, and being responsive and flexible, you can build strong relationships with your customers, increase customer satisfaction, and grow your business over time.

Chapter 28.

Building Strong Community Relationships

Running a successful trucking business requires more than just acquiring customers and hauling freight. It also requires building strong relationships with the communities in which you operate. These relationships can provide many benefits for your business, including increased support and favorable publicity. Here are some tips for building strong community relationships.

Get Involved in the Community

One of the best ways to build strong relationships with the community is to get involved. This can be done by participating in local events, sponsoring local sports teams, or volunteering with local organizations. By becoming a visible part of the community, you will be better able to understand the needs and concerns of the people who live there. This will also give you the opportunity to show them the positive impact your business can have on the community.

Be a Good Neighbor

Another important aspect of building strong community relationships is being a good neighbor. This means following local regulations, respecting the rights of others, and being considerate of your neighbors. For example, if you have a trucking business that requires a lot of parking for vehicles, make sure you are not taking up too much space or blocking driveways.

Support Local Causes

Supporting local causes can be a great way to build strong relationships with the community. This can be done by making donations, volunteering time, or participating in local fundraising events. By supporting local causes, you are showing your commitment to the community and helping to make a positive impact.

Be Accessible and Responsive

It is important to be accessible and responsive to your customers and the community. This means being available to answer questions and address concerns, as well as being prompt in responding to requests. By being accessible and responsive, you are demonstrating your commitment to providing excellent customer service and building strong relationships.

In conclusion, building strong community relationships is an important part of running a successful trucking business. By getting involved in the community, being a good neighbor, supporting local causes, being accessible and responsive, and demonstrating your commitment to providing excellent customer service, you can create positive relationships that will benefit your business in the long term.

Chapter 29.

Diversifying Your Business

As a trucking business owner, it's important to always be looking for ways to grow and expand your operations. One effective strategy for doing so is to diversify your business. By offering additional services or products, you can tap into new markets and increase your revenue streams. In this chapter, we'll discuss some ways you can diversify your trucking business.

1. Offer Logistics and Supply Chain Management Services

One way to diversify your trucking business is to offer logistics and supply chain management services to your customers. This involves helping companies manage their entire supply chain, from sourcing raw materials to delivering finished goods to the end customer. By offering these services, you can help companies streamline their operations, increase efficiency, and reduce costs.

2. Provide Delivery Services for Other Businesses

Another way to diversify your trucking business is to offer delivery services for other businesses. This could involve delivering products for other companies, such as food, clothing, or electronics. By doing so, you can increase your revenue streams and tap into new markets.

3. Offer Specialty Services

If you have specialized equipment or experience, you can offer specialty services to your customers. For example, you could offer flatbed trucking services for over-sized loads, or refrigerated trucking services for perishable goods. By doing so, you can differentiate yourself from your competitors and attract customers who are looking for specialized services.

4. Expand into International Markets

Expanding your trucking business into international markets can also be a way to diversify your operations. By doing so, you can tap into new markets and increase your revenue streams. However, it's important to be aware of the challenges involved in expanding internationally, such as navigating different regulations and cultural differences.

5. Partner with Other Businesses

Partnering with other businesses can also be a way to diversify your trucking business. For example, you could partner with a logistics company to offer end-to-end supply chain management services to your customers. By doing so, you can leverage each other's strengths and offer a wider range of services to your customers.

6. Develop New Products

Finally, you can diversify your trucking business by developing new products. For example, you could develop a GPS tracking system specifically for trucking companies, or you could create a software platform to help companies manage their logistics operations. By developing new products, you can tap into new markets and increase your revenue streams.

In conclusion, diversifying your trucking business can help you grow and expand your operations. By offering new services or products, you can tap into new markets and increase your revenue streams. However, it's important to carefully consider the challenges involved in diversifying your business and to ensure that you have the resources and expertise to succeed.

Chapter 30.

Attracting and Retaining Drivers

Attracting and Retaining Drivers: A Key Element of a Successful Trucking Business

When it comes to running a successful trucking business, there are a number of key components that need to be in place. One of the most important of these components is a talented and motivated team of drivers. After all, your drivers are the ones who are actually out on the road, delivering your freight and representing your company. So, how do you go about attracting and retaining top-quality drivers?

First, it's important to understand that there are a number of factors that can influence a driver's decision to join your company and stay with it. These factors can include things like pay and benefits, work-life balance, the quality of the equipment they'll be driving, the level of support they'll receive from management and dispatch, and the reputation of the company within the industry.

With that in mind, here are some specific strategies you can use to attract and retain drivers:

1. Offer competitive pay and benefits. Pay and benefits are some of the most important factors drivers consider when deciding whether or not to join a company. Make sure you're offering a competitive salary and benefits package that takes into account the cost of living in your area and the current market rates for drivers in your industry. Consider offering things like health

insurance, paid time off, and 401(k) matching to make your company even more attractive.

2. Provide quality equipment. Drivers want to know that they'll be driving safe and reliable trucks, and that they'll have access to the tools and equipment they need to do their job effectively. Make sure your vehicles are well-maintained, and invest in the latest technology and safety features to give your drivers peace of mind.

3. Foster a supportive and inclusive company culture. Drivers want to feel like they're part of a team and that they're valued and appreciated for the hard work they do. Make sure your management and dispatch teams are supportive and respectful, and encourage open communication and collaboration across all levels of the company.

4. Offer work-life balance. Long hours on the road can be tough, and drivers need time to rest and recharge. Offer flexible scheduling options and promote a healthy work-life balance by encouraging drivers to take breaks and get the rest they need.

5. Invest in training and development. Drivers want to know that they're growing and developing professionally, and that they're being given the tools they need to succeed. Offer ongoing training and development opportunities, and provide drivers with access to the latest technologies and best practices in the industry.

6. Promote your company. Use social media, your website, and other marketing channels to promote your

company and highlight why it's a great place to work. Share positive stories from your drivers, and use testimonials to showcase the benefits of working for your company.

7. Offer incentives and rewards. A little recognition and appreciation can go a long way in motivating drivers and keeping them engaged. Consider offering incentives and rewards for things like safe driving, meeting delivery targets, and excellent customer service.

By implementing these strategies, you can create a company culture that is attractive to top-quality drivers, and one that will help you retain your best drivers for years to come. And by doing so, you'll be setting yourself up for long-term success in the trucking industry.

Chapter 31.

Navigating Labor Relations

Navigating Labor Relations: A Guide for Your Trucking Business

As a trucking business owner, you want to create a harmonious work environment for your employees and drivers. This is crucial for not only ensuring that your business runs smoothly, but also for attracting and retaining the best talent. One important aspect of building a positive work environment is managing labor relations effectively.

The first step in navigating labor relations is to have a clear understanding of labor laws and regulations. This includes knowledge of minimum wage laws, overtime requirements, and workplace safety regulations. Staying up-to-date on these laws can help you avoid costly penalties and lawsuits. Additionally, it's important to have a clear policy in place for resolving disputes and handling employee grievances.

In order to build positive labor relations, it's important to communicate openly and honestly with your employees. This means taking the time to listen to their concerns and working together to find solutions that work for everyone. It also means being transparent about company policies and procedures, and being willing to make changes when necessary to create a better work environment.

Another important aspect of labor relations is employee relations. This involves creating a culture that encourages teamwork, collaboration, and mutual respect between employees and drivers. This can be achieved through regular team-building activities, open forums for employee feedback, and promoting a sense of community within the workplace.

Another key aspect of labor relations is developing fair and equitable compensation and benefits packages for employees. This includes not only fair wages, but also benefits such as health insurance, paid time off, and retirement savings plans. Offering these benefits can help to attract and retain the best employees, and can also increase employee morale and job satisfaction.

It's also important to have a strong human resources department that can handle employee relations and labor relations issues effectively. This includes having a clear process in place for handling disputes, managing employee benefits and compensation, and ensuring that company policies are being followed.

In addition to these internal efforts, it can be helpful to seek the guidance of a professional labor relations consultant. These experts can provide valuable advice and support on a variety of labor relations issues, from negotiations with unions to resolving workplace disputes.

Finally, it's important to be proactive in promoting positive labor relations. This can be achieved by regularly conducting employee surveys, holding focus groups, and encouraging open communication between employees and management. By taking these steps, you can create a work environment that is supportive, fair, and respectful, which in turn can help to attract and retain the best employees and build a successful trucking business.

In conclusion, managing labor relations is an essential aspect of running a successful trucking business. By understanding labor laws and regulations, communicating openly with employees, and promoting a positive work environment, you can build strong relationships with your employees and create a harmonious workplace. With the right support and resources, you can navigate labor relations with confidence and create a thriving trucking business.

Chapter 32.

Managing Equipment Leasing and Rentals

As a trucking business owner, you have a lot of decisions to make when it comes to your fleet. One of the biggest decisions you'll face is whether to buy or lease your vehicles and equipment. Both options have their pros and cons, and the right choice for your business will depend on a number of factors, including your budget, the size of your fleet, and your long-term plans.

If you choose to lease your equipment, there are a number of factors to consider to make sure you get the best deal possible. First, it's important to understand the different types of leases available. There are two main types of leases: operating leases and capital leases.

Operating leases are a popular option for trucking businesses because they offer a lot of flexibility. With an operating lease, you pay a monthly fee to use the equipment, and at the end of the lease, you have the option to return it or purchase it. This is a great option for businesses that are just starting out and need to keep their costs low. It's also a good choice for businesses that want to upgrade their equipment frequently, as operating leases usually have a shorter term.

Capital leases are similar to a loan, where you make payments to own the equipment. Capital leases usually have a longer term and a lower monthly payment, but at the end of the lease, you own the equipment outright. This is a good option for businesses that have a large fleet and want to own their equipment outright, but it's important to make sure you have the budget to make the larger payments over a longer period of time.

Another important factor to consider when leasing equipment is the lease agreement itself. Make sure you understand all of the terms and conditions, including the length of the lease, the monthly payment, and any penalties for early termination. It's also important to make sure the lease agreement includes maintenance and repair provisions, so you know who will be responsible for fixing any issues that arise during the lease period.

When negotiating a lease, it's important to keep in mind that the lessor (the person or company who owns the equipment) wants to make a profit, and the lessee (you) wants to keep costs low. It's a good idea to work with a lawyer to make sure you understand all of the terms and conditions and to negotiate a lease that works for both parties.

Finally, when considering leasing, it's important to think about the long-term implications. Leasing may seem like the more affordable option in the short-term, but in the long-term, it can be more expensive than owning the equipment outright. Make sure you take a close look at the total cost of ownership, including interest payments, and weigh the benefits and drawbacks of both options before making a decision.

In conclusion, managing equipment leasing and rentals is a critical part of running a successful trucking business. By understanding the different types of leases available, negotiating a fair lease agreement, and thinking about the long-term implications, you can make an informed decision that will help your business grow and succeed.

Chapter 33.

Staying Ahead of Industry Trends

Running a successful trucking business is a challenging and ever-evolving endeavor. The industry is constantly changing, and it's important to stay ahead of the curve to stay ahead of the competition and thrive. Here are some tips for staying ahead of industry trends:

1. Stay informed about new technologies The trucking industry is rapidly advancing with new technologies. From telematics to electric trucks, it's important to stay informed about new technologies and how they can improve your business. Keeping up with the latest advancements will give you an edge and increase efficiency and productivity.

2. Network with industry leaders and experts Networking with other trucking business owners, industry leaders, and experts can be a great way to stay informed about industry trends. Attend industry conferences, trade shows, and other events to learn from experts and make new connections. Joining industry associations can also be a great way to stay informed and network with others in the industry.

3. Analyze industry data and trends Monitoring industry data and trends can help you make informed decisions about your business. Keep an eye on trucking industry reports, shipping and logistics trends, and other relevant data to stay ahead of the curve. This information can help you make informed decisions

about pricing, route planning, and other important aspects of your business.

4. Invest in employee training and education Investing in employee training and education is a great way to stay ahead of industry trends. Encourage your employees to attend industry conferences and training sessions, and invest in their education. This will not only help them stay informed about the latest advancements, but it will also improve their job performance and satisfaction.

5. Embrace new and innovative solutions The trucking industry is full of innovative solutions that can help you stay ahead of the curve. From automated dispatch systems to fuel-efficient engines, embracing new solutions can help you increase efficiency and save money. It's important to stay open-minded and willing to try new solutions to stay ahead of the competition.

6. Focus on sustainability Sustainability is becoming increasingly important in the trucking industry. Companies that embrace sustainable practices, such as reducing their carbon footprint and using eco-friendly fuels, are more likely to attract customers and stay ahead of the competition. Investing in sustainable solutions, such as electric trucks, can help you reduce costs and increase efficiency while doing your part to protect the environment.

In conclusion, staying ahead of industry trends is essential for success in the trucking industry. By staying informed about new technologies, networking with industry experts, analyzing industry data, investing in employee training, embracing new solutions, focusing on sustainability, and more, you can stay ahead of the competition and thrive in the ever-evolving trucking industry.

Chapter 34.

Utilizing Analytics and Performance Metrics

As a trucking business owner, it's important to stay informed and up-to-date on industry trends, as well as the performance of your own operations. This information can be critical in helping you make informed decisions about the future of your business, and in identifying areas for improvement. In order to achieve this, it's essential to make use of data and analytics.

There are many different metrics and KPIs (Key Performance Indicators) that you can use to monitor the performance of your business. Some of the most important metrics for a trucking business include:

- Load utilization: This metric measures how effectively you're utilizing the capacity of your vehicles. By tracking this metric, you can identify opportunities to optimize your routes and increase your efficiency.

- Fuel efficiency: Monitoring fuel efficiency is critical for controlling costs. This metric helps you track how much fuel your vehicles are consuming, and identify areas where you can improve your fuel consumption and save money.

- Driver performance: Tracking your drivers' performance is an important part of managing your business. You can use metrics such as miles driven, hours worked, and safety records to monitor their performance and identify areas where they need additional training or support.

- Customer satisfaction: Keeping your customers happy is essential for the success of your business. You can use metrics such as delivery time, on-time delivery rate, and complaint resolution time to monitor customer satisfaction and identify areas for improvement.

There are many different tools and software solutions available to help you track these metrics and KPIs. Some of the most popular options include:

- Fleet management software: Fleet management software can provide real-time data and analytics on your vehicles, drivers, and operations. You can use this software to monitor your performance, track your KPIs, and make informed decisions about the future of your business.

- Data analytics tools: Data analytics tools can help you process and analyze large amounts of data, and identify trends and patterns in your operations. You can use these tools to gain valuable insights into your business, and make data-driven decisions about the future of your operations.

- Business intelligence software: Business intelligence software can provide you with a comprehensive view of your business, and help you make informed decisions about the future of your operations. This software can help you track and analyze your performance, monitor your KPIs, and gain valuable insights into your business.

By making use of these tools and software solutions, you can stay ahead of the competition and make informed decisions about the future of your trucking business. Here are a few tips to help you get started:

1. Identify the most important metrics and KPIs for your business. Start by determining which metrics and KPIs are most relevant to your business, and focus on tracking and analyzing these first.

2. Choose the right tools and software solutions for your business. Consider your budget, the size of your business, and your specific needs when selecting the tools and software solutions that will work best for you.

3. Make data-driven decisions. Use the data and insights you gain from your analytics and performance metrics to make informed decisions about the future of your business.

4. Continuously monitor and refine your metrics and KPIs. As your business evolves and grows, you'll need to continuously monitor and refine your metrics and KPIs to ensure that you're tracking the most relevant information.

In conclusion, utilizing analytics and performance metrics is a crucial aspect of any trucking business. By tracking key metrics, you can make informed decisions that will help your business grow and succeed. There are many different tools and technologies available to help you collect and analyze data, from simple spreadsheets to sophisticated data management platforms. The key is to find the right tools for your business and to use them consistently and effectively.

Performance metrics such as fuel efficiency, driver utilization, and on-time delivery rates can give you valuable insight into the performance of your operations and help you identify areas for improvement. By setting clear goals and tracking your progress over time, you can ensure that your business stays on track and continues to grow.

Additionally, using analytics can help you make informed decisions about your marketing strategy, route planning, and customer service. You can use data to understand your customers better, identify trends and patterns, and develop targeted marketing campaigns that will help you reach your target audience.

Finally, by using analytics to measure and improve the performance of your operations, you can stay ahead of the competition and remain competitive in a rapidly evolving industry. Whether you're a small fleet owner or a large logistics company, incorporating analytics into your business strategy will help you succeed and grow.

Chapter 35.

Managing and Reducing Operating Costs

As a business owner in the trucking industry, managing and reducing operating costs is a critical component of success. The trucking business is heavily reliant on fuel, labor, and equipment expenses, which can quickly eat away at profit margins if not properly managed. However, with a strategic approach, it is possible to reduce costs, increase efficiency, and ultimately boost the bottom line.

Here are some tips to help you manage and reduce operating costs in your trucking business:

1. Optimize Fleet Utilization: One of the biggest costs in the trucking industry is the cost of the fleet itself. To reduce costs, it is essential to optimize the utilization of your vehicles. Make sure you are getting the most out of each vehicle by maximizing load capacity and scheduling routes effectively. Consider using technology to streamline dispatch and communications and improve route planning.

2. Manage Fuel Costs: Fuel is a significant expense for trucking businesses, but there are ways to reduce costs. Start by monitoring fuel consumption and looking for ways to improve efficiency. Consider implementing fuel-saving technologies such as aerodynamic devices, anti-idling solutions, and efficient engines. You can also negotiate with fuel suppliers to get the best possible prices.

3. Implement Cost-Saving Measures: Consider implementing cost-saving measures such as reducing idle time, using fuel-efficient vehicles, and reducing maintenance costs. You can also look into alternative fuel sources, such as electric or natural gas, which may be more cost-effective in the long run.

4. Monitor and Manage Labor Costs: Labor costs can also be a major drain on resources, so it's important to keep an eye on them. Start by implementing a driver incentive program, which can help attract and retain drivers, reduce turnover, and improve morale. Consider also implementing technology solutions that can streamline dispatch and communications, which can help reduce labor costs and improve efficiency.

5. Evaluate and Negotiate Contracts: Review all contracts with suppliers, partners, and service providers to identify areas where you can negotiate better terms or find more cost-effective solutions. Make sure you are getting the best possible prices for goods and services, and that you are not paying for anything you don't need.

6. Use Analytics and Performance Metrics: Utilize analytics and performance metrics to identify areas of your business that may be contributing to higher operating costs. This data can help you identify areas where you can improve efficiency, reduce waste, and make better-informed decisions. Consider investing in a software solution that can help you monitor and analyze key metrics, such as fuel consumption, vehicle utilization, and labor costs.

7. Seek Professional Advice: If you are unsure about how to manage and reduce operating costs, consider seeking professional advice. Consult with a financial expert or business consultant who can help you identify areas for improvement and provide recommendations for reducing costs.

In conclusion, managing and reducing operating costs is essential for the success of your trucking business. By optimizing fleet utilization, managing fuel costs, implementing cost-saving measures, monitoring labor costs, evaluating and negotiating contracts, utilizing analytics and performance metrics, and seeking professional advice, you can reduce expenses and improve your bottom line. Stay focused and proactive in your approach, and you will be well on your way to success in the trucking industry.

Chapter 36.

Implementing Training and Professional Development Programs

As a trucking business owner, one of your biggest assets is your team. Your drivers, dispatchers, mechanics, and other staff members are the ones who make it all happen, and their success is your success. That's why it's so important to invest in their professional development and training, so they can continue to grow, improve, and add value to your business.

But how do you get started with a training and professional development program for your trucking business? Here are some tips to help you get started:

1. Assess your needs: The first step in creating a training and professional development program is to assess your business's needs. What areas could your team benefit from training in? What skills do they need to improve? What new technology or equipment do they need to learn how to use? Once you have a good understanding of what your team needs, you can start to design your program.

2. Make a plan: Once you know what areas you want to focus on, it's time to make a plan. This could include a combination of in-person training sessions, online courses, workshops, and other opportunities for professional development. Be sure to budget for these activities and make sure you have enough time and resources to implement them effectively.

3. Offer incentives: People are more likely to participate in training and professional development programs if there are incentives involved. Consider offering bonuses, time off, or other rewards for your employees who complete the program or achieve certain milestones. This will not only help to motivate them, but it will also show them that you are committed to their success.

4. Encourage participation: Once your training and professional development program is up and running, make sure your employees know about it and encourage them to participate. Offer flexible scheduling, so they can attend training sessions and workshops without it affecting their work schedule. Encourage open communication, so they feel comfortable asking questions and giving feedback.

5. Continuously evaluate and improve: Finally, it's important to continuously evaluate and improve your training and professional development program. Ask your employees for feedback, and make changes based on what they say. Keep track of the results and make adjustments as needed. This will help you to keep your program relevant, effective, and beneficial for your team.

Investing in the professional development of your team is a win-win situation. Your employees will benefit from the training, and your business will benefit from their improved skills and knowledge. Whether you're just starting out or have been in the trucking business for years, it's never too late to start a training and professional development program. Start today, and you'll see the results in no time.

In conclusion, investing in training and professional development programs is crucial to the success of your business. By empowering your employees with the skills and knowledge they need to perform their jobs effectively, you are not only improving their performance but also contributing to the overall success of your company. Whether through in-house training sessions, online courses, or external workshops and seminars, providing your employees with opportunities for growth and development sends a positive message about your commitment to their success, which can help to improve morale and reduce turnover. Additionally, investing in professional development can help your employees stay ahead of industry trends, which can provide a competitive advantage and position your business for long-term success. Overall, implementing training and professional development programs is an investment in your people, your business, and your future.

Chapter 37.

Building Strong Relationships with Shippers

As a logistics or transportation business, having strong relationships with shippers is crucial to the success of your operations. Shippers are the lifeblood of your business and their needs and preferences must be met in order for you to maintain and grow your customer base. Whether you are an owner-operator or a large fleet, the following tips can help you build and maintain strong relationships with shippers.

1. Communication is Key: Maintaining open lines of communication with your shippers is essential. This means responding to their inquiries promptly, keeping them informed of any changes in the delivery schedule, and providing regular updates on the status of their shipments. Good communication can help build trust and confidence with your shippers, and make them more likely to do business with you again in the future.

2. Offer Competitive Pricing: Pricing is often a major factor in a shipper's decision to use your services. By offering competitive pricing and flexible payment terms, you can attract and retain shippers who are looking for cost-effective and convenient transportation solutions.

3. Provide Reliable and Timely Service: Shippers expect their shipments to be delivered on time and in good condition. By ensuring that your drivers are well-trained and equipped with the necessary tools and technology to get the job done, you can deliver reliable and timely service to your shippers.

4. Invest in Technology: Technology can help you streamline your operations and make them more efficient. By investing in tools such as GPS tracking, electronic logging devices, and real-time communication platforms, you can provide shippers with accurate and up-to-date information about their shipments, which can help build their trust in your services.

5. Build Personal Relationships: Building personal relationships with your shippers can go a long way in fostering trust and loyalty. Take the time to get to know your shippers, understand their business needs, and learn about their products. This can help you better understand their shipping requirements and provide customized solutions that meet their specific needs.

6. Seek Feedback: Regularly seeking feedback from your shippers can help you identify areas for improvement and make necessary changes to your operations. Encouraging shippers to share their opinions and suggestions can help you build a reputation for being responsive and customer-focused, which can attract new business.

7. Resolve Issues Quickly: When issues arise, it is important to resolve them quickly and effectively. By responding promptly to shipper concerns and taking proactive steps to resolve any issues, you can demonstrate your commitment to customer satisfaction and build a reputation for being reliable and trustworthy.

In conclusion, building strong relationships with shippers requires effort, commitment, and a focus on meeting their needs. By following these tips, you can position your business for success and attract and retain loyal customers who will help drive growth and profitability. Remember, building strong relationships takes time and effort, but the payoff can be substantial in terms of increased business, lower costs, and a more positive reputation in the industry.

Chapter 38.

Developing a Succession Plan

As a transportation and logistics business owner, you've likely put in countless hours, hard work, and dedication to build and grow your company. But what happens when it's time to step away from your business and pass the torch to someone else? This is where succession planning comes into play. Succession planning is the process of preparing for the eventual transfer of your business to someone else. Whether it's due to retirement, illness, or any other reason, having a solid succession plan in place can ensure the continued success of your business and protect the investments you've made.

So, where do you start with developing a succession plan? Let's take a look.

1. Identify Your Goals and Objectives

The first step in developing a succession plan is to identify your goals and objectives for your business and your personal life. What do you want to achieve with your business, and what do you hope to accomplish in your personal life once you step away from the company? Understanding your goals and objectives will help you determine the best approach for succession planning.

2. Assess Your Business

Once you have a clear understanding of your goals and objectives, it's time to assess your business. What are its strengths and weaknesses? Who are the key players in your organization, and what roles do they play? What are the critical functions of your business, and how can they be sustained during the transition period? Answering these questions will give you a clear understanding of the areas that need to be addressed in your succession plan.

3. Choose a Successor

Choosing a successor is one of the most important decisions you'll make in your succession plan. It's important to consider the following factors when selecting a successor:

- Experience: Does the potential successor have the experience and skills necessary to run your business effectively?
- Leadership: Does the potential successor have the leadership skills required to lead your employees and keep the company moving in the right direction?
- Alignment with values: Does the potential successor share the same values and vision for the company as you do?

4. Develop a Transition Plan

Once you've chosen a successor, it's time to develop a transition plan. This plan should include the steps and timeline for transferring ownership, responsibility, and decision-making authority from you to the successor. It should also include plans for training and mentoring the successor, as well as a strategy for communicating the transition to employees, customers, and suppliers.

5. Review and Revise Your Plan Regularly

Your succession plan is not a set-it-and-forget-it document. It's important to review and revise it regularly to ensure that it remains relevant and aligned with your goals and objectives. Regular review and revision will also ensure that your plan stays up-to-date with changes in your business, the industry, and your personal life.

Conclusion:

Developing a succession plan is an important step for any transportation and logistics business owner. By identifying your goals and objectives, assessing your business, choosing a successor, developing a transition plan, and reviewing and revising your plan regularly, you can ensure the continued success of your business and protect your investments for years to come. Don't wait until it's too late – start developing your succession plan today.

Chapter 39.

Navigating Legal Issues and Compliance

Running a transportation or logistics business can be a complex and challenging task, especially when it comes to complying with the ever-changing legal landscape. Whether it's dealing with DOT regulations, navigating employment laws, or protecting against liability, it is essential to understand the legal issues that can impact your business. In this chapter, we'll discuss some of the key legal considerations that transportation and logistics businesses should be aware of, and provide tips for staying on top of compliance.

DOT Regulations

The Department of Transportation (DOT) has a range of regulations that apply to transportation and logistics businesses, covering everything from hours of service for drivers to the inspection of commercial vehicles. It is essential to stay up-to-date with the latest DOT regulations and ensure that your business is in compliance with them. One of the key regulations to be aware of is the Federal Motor Carrier Safety Administration's (FMCSA) hours of service (HOS) rules, which dictate the number of hours a driver can spend behind the wheel each day and each week. Non-compliance with HOS regulations can result in fines, penalties, and even legal action.

Employment Laws

Employment laws are another area of legal concern for transportation and logistics businesses. It is essential to understand your obligations as an employer, including minimum wage requirements, overtime regulations, and anti-discrimination laws. It is also important to have clear and concise employment contracts in place that outline the terms and conditions of employment, including job duties, hours of work, and compensation.

Liability

Liability is another critical legal consideration for transportation and logistics businesses. This can include anything from accidents involving your vehicles to damage to cargo during transit. It is essential to have insurance in place to protect your business against liability, and to ensure that your insurance coverage is adequate for the type of operations you are conducting. It is also important to have clear and comprehensive policies and procedures in place to minimize the risk of accidents and minimize the impact of any incidents that do occur.

Compliance Monitoring

Staying compliant with legal regulations can be a complex and time-consuming task, but it is essential to the long-term success of your business. One of the best ways to ensure that your business is in compliance with all relevant regulations is to implement a comprehensive compliance monitoring program. This can include regular reviews of your operations, training for employees, and regular assessments of your compliance with regulations.

Tips for Staying on Top of Compliance

1. Stay informed: Stay up-to-date with the latest legal regulations and requirements, and ensure that your business is in compliance with them.
2. Have clear policies and procedures in place: Ensure that your business has clear and comprehensive policies and procedures in place to minimize the risk of legal issues arising.
3. Implement a compliance monitoring program: Develop and implement a comprehensive compliance monitoring program to ensure that your business stays in compliance with regulations.
4. Work with legal experts: Work with legal experts who understand the transportation and logistics industry, and who can provide guidance and support in navigating legal issues and compliance.
5. Invest in training: Invest in training for your employees, to help ensure that they understand the legal regulations that apply to your business and their role in maintaining compliance.

In conclusion, navigating legal issues and compliance is a critical aspect of running a successful transportation or logistics business. By staying informed, having clear policies and procedures in place, implementing a compliance monitoring program, and working with legal experts, you can help ensure that your business stays compliant with regulations and protects against liability. By taking these steps, you can help ensure the long-term success of your business and stay ahead of the competition.

<u>Chapter 40.</u>

Conclusion

Running a successful trucking business is no easy feat. It requires careful planning, hard work, and a never-ending commitment to improvement. The trucking industry is constantly evolving, and it can be challenging to keep up with the latest trends and best practices. In this guide, we've covered many of the key areas you'll need to focus on to run a successful trucking operation. Whether you're just starting out or looking to take your business to the next level, we hope you've found the information in this guide helpful.

To recap, some of the key areas we've discussed include:

- Maximizing load capacity and utilization
- Implementing technology solutions
- Handling disputes and resolving conflicts
- Expanding your fleet
- Navigating the freight market
- Developing a safety culture
- Staying ahead of the competition
- Streamlining dispatch and communications
- Managing fuel costs and efficiency
- Implementing driver incentives and rewards
- Understanding taxes and recordkeeping
- Building strong relationships with suppliers and partners
- Managing maintenance and repairs
- Improving logistics and supply chain management
- Evaluating and negotiating contracts
- Enhancing customer service
- Building strong community relationships

- Diversifying your business
- Attracting and retaining drivers
- Navigating labor relations
- Managing equipment leasing and rentals
- Staying ahead of industry trends
- Utilizing analytics and performance metrics
- Managing and reducing operating costs
- Implementing training and professional development programs
- Building strong relationships with shippers
- Developing a succession plan
- Navigating legal issues and compliance

Each of these topics is crucial to the success of your trucking business, and it's essential to give them the attention they deserve. Whether you're looking to improve your load utilization, build stronger relationships with your partners, or stay ahead of industry trends, it's essential to have a solid plan in place. By focusing on these key areas and continually working to improve your operation, you'll be well on your way to success.

In conclusion, running a successful trucking business is not an easy task, but it's one that's well worth the effort. By staying up-to-date on the latest trends and best practices, focusing on the key areas that matter most, and continuously working to improve your operation, you'll be able to build a thriving business that you can be proud of. Good luck!

conclusion

operating a successful transportation or logistics business requires a comprehensive approach to managing various aspects of your operations. From maximizing load capacity and utilization, implementing technology solutions, handling disputes and resolving conflicts, expanding your fleet, and navigating the freight market, to developing a safety culture, staying ahead of the competition, streamlining dispatch and communications, managing fuel costs and efficiency, implementing driver incentives and rewards, understanding taxes and recordkeeping, building strong relationships with suppliers and partners, managing maintenance and repairs, improving logistics and supply chain management, evaluating and negotiating contracts, enhancing customer service, building strong community relationships, diversifying your business, attracting and retaining drivers, navigating labor relations, managing equipment leasing and rentals, staying ahead of industry trends, utilizing analytics and performance metrics, managing and reducing operating costs, implementing training and professional development programs, building strong relationships with shippers, and developing a succession plan, it's important to stay organized, focused, and proactive in order to achieve long-term success.

Navigating legal issues and compliance is also critical to ensure that your business operates within the law and protects the interests of all stakeholders involved. With all the best wishes and success, we hope that this book has provided you with valuable insights and practical guidance on how to achieve your goals and build a thriving transportation or logistics business. Whether you're an experienced industry veteran or just starting out, always remember to stay focused, keep learning, and stay ahead of the curve in order to achieve long-term success.

Wishing you all the best in your endeavors!

www.ingramcontent.com/pod-product-compliance
Lightning Source LLC
Chambersburg PA
CBHW071049290526
45795CB00004B/1400

9798880192113